Praise for
Practical Meditation for Beginners

"Ben's keen understanding of meditation and his deep commitment to its practice has given rise to one of the best meditation books I've ever seen. This is a must-read for anyone who is truly interested in learning how to meditate and for those who want to refresh their practice."

Ora Nadrich, author of *Says Who?* and founder of
The Institute For Transformational Thinking

"This book will provide readers with both an excellent road map to begin—or to deepen—their practice as well as a primer on the philosophy, spirituality, and neuroscience behind different meditations styles. It's written with heart, devotion, and dedication to make the ancient teachings available to contemporary meditation students. A wonderful read!"

Ronald Alexander Ph.D., author of *Wise Mind, Open Mind* and
Executive Director of The Open Mind Training Institute

"No one can give us a greater gift than to teach us how to meditate. Many will one day remember Ben Decker as having put their feet on a most joyous path."

Marianne Williamson, author of *A Return to Love*

PRACTICAL
MEDITATION
FOR
BEGINNERS

Practical
Meditation
.... *for* ....
Beginners
10 Days to a Happier,
Calmer You

BENJAMIN W. DECKER

ALTHEA
PRESS

For general information on our other products and services or to obtain technical support, please contact our Customer Care Department within the United States at (866) 744-2665, or outside the United States at (510) 253-0500.

Althea Press publishes its books in a variety of electronic and print formats. Some content that appears in print may not be available in electronic books, and vice versa.

ISBN: Print 978-1-64152-025-6 | eBook 978-1-64152-026-3

For Wyatt, Nolan, Charlie, Audrey, Lincoln, Henry, and all my other nieces and nephews on the way.

CONTENTS

INTRODUCTION

When I was young, I was profoundly struck by how in movies and TV as well as in my family, community, and church life, meditation showed up again and again, always in association with serenity and power. The whole world seemed to be aware of its "mystical" powers to calm and heal the mind. My early fascination with meditation sent me on a learning journey through many traditions—from the Buddhist and Hindu origins of meditation to the Jewish, Islamic, Christian, and even indigenous practices of North and South America—exploring their diverse techniques and practices.

I loved to learn about the ancient philosophers, scientists, saints and sages who discovered some of the most profound truths about existence—including meditation and its many benefits. Time and time again, technology, along with advances in neuroscience and even genetics, seems to be validating things our ancestors knew all along by revealing exactly what happens physiologically during meditation and how regular practice can improve our bodies and minds.

A study by Harvard Medical School neuroscientist Sara Lazar showed meditation was found to physically change the brain, making it more effective in areas associated with learning, mental cognition, memory, and emotional regulation. Numerous other studies have validated these findings and discovered other benefits such as reduced stress, reduced blood pressure, and even increased joy.

My early fascination sent me on a long-term research project. In my teens, I completed a four-year seminary program in my parents' religion, and that was an extraordinary experience. It opened my mind to all the many and varied things I didn't know about the world. I read every book I could get my hands on—books on comparative religion, books on the history of meditation in different cultures, and anything I could find on neuroscience to explore how meditation changes the brain and body. I went to every lecture, workshop, and class on meditation I could find. Over the years, I participated in formal study programs at Deer Park Monastery, The Self-Realization Fellowship, and The Theosophical Society. I participated in silent retreats and meditation challenges, and eventually I found mentors who guided me to explore traditional paths of Zen Buddhism, Taoism, and spiritual psychology through The OpenMind Training Institute and The Institute For Transformational Thinking.

This journey of exploration through the world's traditions and techniques inspired the content of this book, which offers a 10-day meditation program with clear, step-by-step instructions for each of the 10 different meditation practices—one per day—to get you meditating right away.

Through clear instruction and regular practice, meditation will help you experience a deeper connection to your senses, your body, your emotions, and the boundless frontier of your thinking mind. And all you need to start building that connection is a chair or cushion, a quiet place, a timer, and a notebook. That's it! You can begin today.

At the end of the 10 days, you will be familiar with the experience and process of these meditation techniques, and the specific benefits each provides. You can use the program to help you discover the right meditation technique for you, and the one (or two or three) that work best with your individual lifestyle and goals. Based on the foundation this program will build, I can guide you to develop an ongoing meditation practice that you can grow and sustain for years to come.

HOW TO USE THIS BOOK

In Zen there is a word called *shoshin*, or the **beginner's mind**. A beginner's mind allows you to remain flexible and open, even as you encounter new things that may seem strange or even uncomfortable at first. It also allows you to experience something mundane from an entirely new perspective, whereas an expert might approach something believing they "already get it."

My best advice to you on how to successfully progress through this meditation program is to embrace your beginner's mind. Don't judge yourself or your new practice. Using the program in this book, and with me guiding you every step of the way, you will explore meditation practices that have their roots throughout the ages and across the world. Some of the 10 practices will feel very natural to you, while others might be more challenging. Count on your beginner's mind to help you through any times when you might feel resistant or self-conscious about your practice. With a beginner's mind, we can all become more fluid in our understanding and thereby pave the way for a more fulfilling and balanced future.

"In the beginner's mind there are many possibilities; in the expert's mind there are few."

Shunryu Suzuki, from his book *Zen Mind, Beginner's Mind*

It will be very helpful for you to designate a particular time and place to meditate every day for the duration of the program. While this may not be logistically possible for the whole 10 days, I encourage you to set that as your intention, since practicing at the same time every day and in the same quiet place can help eliminate distractions. Most meditations require nothing more than a quiet room and a chair, although for Day 6: Walking Meditation, you will need room to walk around (outdoors is best), and Day 7: Body Scan Meditation is practiced lying down. Keep these logistical things in mind as you plan for the next 10 days.

During this 10-day journey, I place emphasis on the ideas and practices about which the many cultures and traditions represented in this meditation program *agree*. We will take the perspective that anything that generates life or wellness is worthy of exploring and keeping. We will open our minds and hearts to the power of the wisdom of our ancient ancestors while keeping our feet deeply rooted in the modern world.

Research says that it can take as few as four days to experience measurable benefits from meditation, and that it takes anywhere from 21 to 66 days to form a strong habit, depending on what habit you're trying to develop. This means that although at the end of 10 days you may not be dropping to your meditation cushion like clockwork, this program will get you meditating long enough for you to begin to experience the benefits, and the seeds of the habit will be planted. From that point, you'll be able to figure out how you can best fit this new practice into your everyday life.

I recommend that you follow the program straight through, as written, without skipping a day. Ten days is long enough to really get a taste of meditation and its psychological and physiological benefits but short enough that most people—even really busy people—should be able to commit to it.

Granted, life can still get in the way. If you do have to skip a day, it's not the end of the world, so don't feel bad. However, to build the skills in a logical order and strengthen your meditation habit, the sooner you pick up the practice again after missing a day, the better. If you end up skipping multiple days, consider going back and starting again from Day 1.

Feel free to take a look through the different practices in the book before you start the program. This program is designed to provide you with everything you need to know to begin developing a meditation practice *today*. Each day I'll introduce you to a variation of meditation that places emphasis on a different technique. Buy a small notebook or journal and have it on hand when you meditate. This Meditation Notebook will be a place to track your progress as you build your new practice, make note of which techniques you liked or maybe struggled with, and respond to the short writing prompts I provide at the end of each chapter. You'll also find steps to take each technique deeper, and additional resources are listed if you want to take your study further.

I know that to a beginner, 10 meditations may seem like a lot. You may be wondering why 10 different techniques are represented and whether that will make things more complicated. The short answer is no, because all meditation, regardless of its style or tradition, teaches the same basic skills: concentration, focus, awareness, and self-regulation. So, over the course of the program, you'll be learning these same core skills, just using different strategies to get there.

Variety is the spice of life, so I also hope that exposing you to a range of techniques will make the program more engaging and fun. Sitting for meditation is the classic technique for a reason: Being physically still can help you still your mind. However, as I mentioned before, it is by no means the only way to meditate, and I want you to taste the fuller range of what a practice can offer. For example, you might be a person who hates to sit still and absolutely under no circumstances wants to sit silently for 20 minutes a day. If that's the case, then Walking Meditation, an ancient practice we'll explore on Day 6, might be just the thing for you. Alternatively, you might find that stillness helps you develop a deep, mindful awareness. The only way to find out which techniques are best for you is to try them out. In my years as a meditation teacher, I've worked with thousands of clients in developing a meditation practice that's right for their personalities, lifestyles, and needs and have found this approach of trying out numerous styles to be the most fun and effective way to help new meditators find the right practice for them.

Throughout the book, you will see **bolded** words and phrases. These are specialized terms that may be unfamiliar to beginning meditators, and so we have defined them in the glossary at the back of the book.

Please keep in mind that some of these meditation practices will feel more comfortable to you than others, and that's why trying a range of techniques is so beneficial. If there's a meditation style you find especially challenging, or just plain don't like, you can skip that one and simply repeat the previous day's meditation. Just be sure to make a note in your Meditation Notebook about what didn't resonate for you with the practice you skipped. This will help you build the ongoing routine that works best for you.

Let's begin!

Zazen Breath Awareness Meditation

MEDITATION LENGTH: 5 MINUTES

What Is It?

Because of its depth, simplicity, and popularity in the United States and other Western countries, we begin with a modern version of the Zen Buddhist practice **zazen**, which is the Zen practice of seated meditation.

Zen, as a school of Buddhist teachings, was founded in China 1,500 years ago. It is said that the Buddhist monk Bodhidharma first spread Buddhism in China, and the teachings meshed well with the Taoist philosophical tradition already practiced there. A Chinese brand of Buddhism was born, and as a result, Zen Buddhism is uniquely Chinese (as opposed to Indian Buddhist schools, which remain closer to their Hindu roots).

In the modern world, there seems to be a collective understanding of the word *Zen*—it has become synonymous with serenity, relaxation, and a calm demeanor. Popularized in the West by Buddhist scholar and theosophist D. T. Suzuki, it's important to recognize that Zen itself is not a religion, a philosophy, or even a practice. As twentieth-century philosopher Alan Watts says in his book *The Way of Zen*, "Zen is . . .

a 'way of liberation'" and posits that it is compatible with every religious tradition.

Unlike many other traditions, in Zen, emphasis is placed on the **direct experience** of **enlightenment**—experiencing insight through meditation—rather than on the study of the sacred texts of Eastern traditions.

Zazen is a great technique to start with because it is so straightforward and uncomplicated. Simply stated, the practice consists of observing your breath. Attention focused on the breath redirects your awareness from outside your body to inside it. It is an exercise in controlling the focus of your awareness. Gradually and naturally (with practice), your awareness will expand from an isolated focus on the breath to a broader focus on bodily sensations and the physical experience, awareness of thoughts, and the impulses *behind* sensation and thought. You'll experience this broader awareness beginning to unfold later in our meditation program. This will eventually enable you to view circumstances and personal experiences from a larger perspective—and it all starts with simply maintaining conscious focus on your breath.

Think of this sitting meditation as a journey through stages of awareness. We first experience ourselves in a safe, calm, peaceful environment. Then we feel what the moment feels like, starting with the body, where tension is felt, where warmth, expansion, nervousness, or excitement is held.

One 5-minute session of zazen practice can have lingering effects of calmness, clarity, and increased attention that last anywhere from an hour up to a full day. In zazen, you create the conditions for your mind to "decompress" from its habitual mode of thinking and open up to new perspectives and insight. This is also true in other forms of meditation, as you will soon find out.

Even 5 minutes can be powerful, but long-term practice of zazen (or any meditation technique) is really where the magic happens. Zazen can ultimately retrain your mind to see the world from an entirely new perspective, allowing your approach to life to become gradually more balanced and richer with meaning. Zazen practice develops our understanding of our connectedness to the world into which we were born, the world in which we live—which is also the world we are creating together, moment by moment.

What You'll Get Out of It

Zen is an especially intriguing school of Buddhism because it brings to mind paradoxical images of monks happily living quiet lives, meditating on mountaintops, as well as powerful martial artists like pop-culture icon Bruce Lee, who was a practitioner of Zen.

As part of a training I once offered for meditation teachers, we visited Deer Park Monastery in Southern California, founded by the renowned Zen monk Thich Nhat Hanh. Among many fond memories of that trip, I recall a number of students remarking how surprised they were at the simplicity of monastic life. It was a true challenge for many of them to experience even just a few hours without the stimulation of their phones and the outside world—and these were experienced meditators! The monks find comfort, contentment, and even joy in the simplest of tasks, living each moment to its fullest by grounding themselves in the present.

In the ever-accelerating modern world, with new technology constantly bombarding our senses and demanding schedules pulling us in different directions, the benefits of a practice like zazen are easy to overlook but profoundly powerful to practice.

By practicing Zazen Breath Awareness Meditation, you will cultivate:

Focus Because your only true *task* in this meditation is to be aware of your breath, this practice will increase your capacity to focus your attention with laser-like precision on whatever it is you choose to focus on. A classic example is the Zen warrior who is able to catch a fly with her chopsticks, barely moving a muscle and never opening her eyes.

Patience Slowly and steadily, as the rush to "gain the benefits" of meditation fades away and the depth of the experience itself becomes apparent, your patience will strengthen and your need to be "moving on to the next moment" will begin to recede.

Clarity As the grounding effect of **breath awareness** disengages you from the often-overwhelming chatter of the mind, the level at which you think will seem to **transcend** the noise. Your awareness will rise above the level of the thoughts that once held you captive, and you'll begin to see things clearly, from a more expansive perspective.

Mind-body connection The chronic tension the average person experiences in modern life finds its way deep into the body, and we live most of our lives in the "whiplash" of past experiences—mentally rehashing and physically re-experiencing past stressors. The practice of breath awareness relieves this tension by shifting attention to the present, and the mental pressures of worries, concerns, and ambitions lift. With focus and practice, you'll become sensitive to the many **microchanges** occurring within the body with every inhale and every exhale.

Self-awareness Similar to the mind-body connection, you'll develop a deeper relationship with your own mind, your own thoughts, and your own emotional states through focused attention.

Self-regulation Your newly developed self-awareness will provide a more direct perception of your physical and mental reactions to your life experiences as you gradually become less attached to the stories you tell yourself about your feelings and thoughts ("I am angry because he mistreated me," for example) and more in touch with the simple presence of the feelings and thoughts themselves. As a result, you'll begin to see your role in different circumstances, recognize your opportunities to grow, and develop a relationship with yourself that is more loving, forgiving, and open to new possibilities.

Joy Appreciating the simple things, the great temporary gift of life and the beauty in all aspects of living, is perhaps one of the most powerful, fulfilling benefits of practicing breath awareness. By choosing to become aware, you choose to take back control of your attention and perspective, which can transform even mundane tasks, such as washing dishes or making coffee, into something joyful and beautiful.

What You'll Need

For today's meditation, as with all meditation techniques, you don't need much to get you going. Whether you sit on the floor or a chair is up to you and often depends on where you decide to practice—home, work, etc. Each day may be different as well, depending on how you're feeling. Today you will need:

- a comfortable chair or cushion where you can sit with your spine comfortably erect

- a quiet place to sit where you won't be easily disturbed (by someone walking in on you, for example)

- a timer (if you decide to use the timer on your smartphone, it is best to put the phone on airplane mode or silent to prevent distractions from incoming alerts)

- your Meditation Notebook and a pen or pencil

WHAT SHOULD I DO WITH MY HANDS?

The key with your hands is to allow them to rest in a comfortable position. You can sit with your hands clasped, palms on your thighs, or palms open on your knees, whatever is most comfortable. But what about those elegant gestures in the ancient paintings of the Buddha or Hindu deities? Those are called **mudras**, and there are hundreds of such hand postures for meditation. They are said to have a powerful impact on your nervous system, generating certain kinds of energy and specific benefits such as alertness, healing, or protection. Here are three you might want to try:

 **GYAN MUDRA** (also known as the om mudra) is used for relaxation and to focus the mind on the task of meditation.

 **DHYANA MUDRA** (most often used by the Buddha) is the mudra for perfect balance and equanimity.

 **SHUNI MUDRA** is used for spiritual and emotional purposes and is also the mudra for cultivating patience.

Get Started

We've all seen the image of the immortal Zen master sitting with his legs crossed like a pretzel and levitating in the enlightened meditative state of **samadi**. While you're absolutely welcome to hold this as an eventual goal, it definitely isn't where we begin! Many traditions have a lot to say about posture, the body's center of energy, and the energy flow throughout the body and its relationship to the environment and your mental alertness. But when you're first starting your practice, you should keep things simple until you find the best posture for you.

In Zen, there are three recommended **asanas**, or postures. Before I explain them, I'd like to make it clear that for our purposes, we will focus on these two recommendations when it comes to posture:

1. Sit in a position that is comfortable enough for you to easily maintain it for the duration of the practice.

2. Avoid postures that are so comfortable you could fall asleep.

I was introduced to meditation as a young child, and my younger brother and I used to practice together. He was my first best friend and also my first student. At the time, I was about eight years old, and he was about five. We loved bending our agile, flexible bodies, and I always loved to show off my perfect lotus posture to the amazement of the adults around me.

As I grew older, my lotus gradually became a half lotus, which was much less impressive. When I was in my early twenties, I read Paramahansa Yogananda's book *Autobiography of a Yogi*, in which he describes the inability of his new American students to sit in true yogic postures. He began to teach his students to meditate sitting upright in a chair—which came as a great relief to me, because when I began his two-year training, my full lotus was long gone! Don't get frustrated with yourself or intimidated by the advanced postures you see on meditation

THE THREE ZAZEN POSTURES

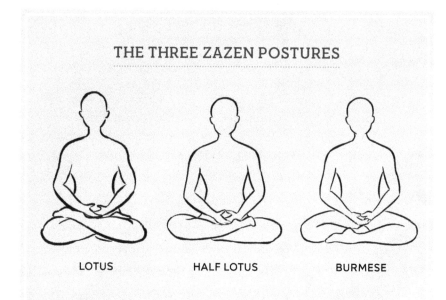

LOTUS   HALF LOTUS   BURMESE

blogs or in yoga magazines. It isn't necessary to sit like that, and this is *your* practice—finding what works for you is part of the process.

As you meditate, your mind will wander. Again, don't judge yourself harshly when it happens. If your mind wanders, all that means is that you're alive and your brain is functioning normally, which is great news! An analogy that has always been helpful for me in understanding the role of the wandering mind in meditation is weight-training exercises. When you're weight training, your goal isn't to become a competitive physique model during your first trip to the gym. The goal is to *actually do* the training. Every time the mind wanders away from the awareness of the breath, notice that it has wandered and bring your awareness back to the breath. This can be likened to a rep in the gym—every time you bring your mind back, you are building your muscle of attention. Your mind wanders, you bring it back. This is the exercise—and the practice—of meditation.

Thoughts are the input and output of the mental process. Making thoughts is what the brain is built for—like the heart beats, the mind thinks. As long as the body is alive and functioning normally, thoughts will take place on one level or another. Be aware that the concept here is to shift your focus to the *awareness* of the thinking process, rather than the *content* of the thoughts.

One of the most common misconceptions about Zen is related to the concept of **no-thought,** which many people think is the goal of all meditation. But no-thought is not as straightforward as those words make it seem. Achieving the advanced state of no-thought is not about stopping the thinking process, but rather, it's about cultivating an expansive sensitivity to a level above the thinking mind. One helpful tip with this is called **mental noting.** When a thought comes to mind, note the thought and return to the practice. Notice where your mind goes when it wanders—"Oh, I'm thinking about work"—then bring your focus back to the breath.

> *"Like lightning all thoughts come and pass."*
> Zen Master Manzan Dohaku

Now, to the practice!

Please read through this entire meditation before beginning. Ideally you will remember the instructions and not have to interrupt the meditation to check the next step.

ZAZEN BREATH AWARENESS MEDITATION

BEFORE MEDITATING

1. Find a place to sit where you won't be disturbed.

2. Take a moment to get into a comfortable position that you will be able to maintain for the duration of the practice with as little movement or adjustment as possible.

3. Set your intention: "I will practice breath awareness as a form of meditation for five minutes, counting each breath. When my mind wanders, I will return to counting the breath, beginning again with one."

BEGIN MEDITATING

1. Set your timer for five minutes.

2. Allow your eyes to gently close.

3. Bring your awareness to the breath.

4. Feel your breath as your lungs expand and contract.

5. Avoid controlling or changing the breath; simply observe it.

6. Count each inhale until you reach 10, then begin again with one.

7. Notice the movement of the body during each breath: the expansion and contraction of the lungs, the movement of the rib cage, and all the other parts of the body that move with the breath.

8. Whenever you lose count (and you probably will), simply begin your counting again, starting with one. The counting is just a way to keep you focused.

When your timer goes off, if you're ready to finish your meditation, take a deep breath and grab your Meditation Notebook. If you have time to sit longer, hit the snooze button or reset your timer and meditate for a few more minutes.

Wrap Up

Make a mental note of how you feel, then take a moment to record your meditation. This will help you track your progress as you work toward your goal of meditating every day for this program's 10 days—and beyond!

You can use the blank lines provided at the end of each chapter if all you have time for is to jot down the basics (date, time, place, and how long you meditated). But it's helpful to have your Meditation Notebook when you want to go deeper or respond to these writing prompts:

- How did your meditation feel?

- What kinds of thoughts came to mind?

- What might you do differently next time you practice this same meditation technique—posture, mudra, length?

- Did you notice anything unexpected about your physical experience?

Go Deeper

Count the exhale rather than the inhale

Begin with the same instructions as above, but try counting each exhale rather than each inhale.

Observe your breath without counting

Notice changes and sensations throughout your body. We will go into more detail about this practice on Day 7: Body Scan Meditation.

Sit longer

The typical recommendation for this technique is 20 to 40 minutes up to twice daily.

Go deeper throughout your day: Stop thinking

This is an additional exercise to take with you throughout your day, to help you reduce mind wandering and bring your awareness to whatever it is that you are doing.

- **Stop thinking**—about anything other than what you are doing right now. Notice your breath. Enjoy all that there is to this moment.

- **Stop thinking**—about your upcoming plans when you take time to read. Notice your breath. Take in each word and allow the information and ideas to settle in.

- **Stop thinking**—about what you are going to say next while someone else is still speaking. Notice your breath. Hear them out, open your mind, and *listen*.

- **Stop thinking**—about all the things that could go wrong in your career. Notice your breath. Be your best and do your best.

- **Stop thinking**—about your workday when you are with your family. Notice your breath. Love them now.

Recommended Reading

Zen Mind, Beginner's Mind by Shunryu Suzuki

The Way of Zen by Alan W. Watts

The Zen Teaching of Bodhidharma by Bodhidharma

Zen and the Art of Motorcycle Maintenance by Robert M. Pirsig

Jeet Kune Do: Bruce Lee's Commentaries on the Martial Way by Bruce Lee

NOTES: DAY 1

Date: .... Time: ....

Length of meditation: ....

Posture: ....

Mudra used (if applicable): ....

In a few words (e.g., easy, challenging, relaxing, boring) describe how you found the meditation:

....

....

....

....

....

....

Open Awareness Meditation

MEDITATION LENGTH: 5 MINUTES

What Is It?

Open Awareness Meditation, also known as "open attention," "open monitoring," or "**soft focus,**" is a form of **mindfulness meditation** in which you allow the many things present in your consciousness (sounds and other sensory input, as well as your thoughts and emotions) to arise in your awareness and then naturally fall away as they are replaced by different sounds, thoughts, etc. This kind of meditation is considered a "yin" practice.

The ancient concept of **yin and yang** refers to the two fundamental sides of nature—both spiritual and physical, both feminine and masculine. This does not refer exclusively to male or female, but to the masculine and feminine in all aspects of life. *Yin* is the feminine aspect of all things and is associated with that which is expansive, open, and receptive, while *yang* is the masculine aspect of all things and is associated with that which is precise, active, and specific. Every person has both yin qualities and yang qualities, and the same is true of meditation practices. As you progress through the program, you will find that each practice contains elements of both, while often emphasizing one quality more than the other.

Attention is the yin to concentration's yang. Attention (mindfulness) and concentration (focus) work together to provide a full, rounded experience of being both focused on the task at hand (whatever it may be), as well as having a complete awareness of, and an open mind to, the many aspects of the moment you are in.

In most meditation practices, you will be exercising some level of both concentration *and* open attention.

The Mindfulness Sutras (or the Satipatthana Suttas, as they are known in their original language, Pali) are the primary foundational texts for what we know today as **mindfulness** and mindfulness meditation. Mindfulness refers to the experience of being totally aware of all the information your senses are processing. In the Eastern traditions, there are six natural senses that all humans are born with. This includes the five conventional senses—sight, hearing, smell, taste, and touch—and the sixth sense, *thought*. This sixth sense of thought often comes to the foreground in mindfulness practices and in meditation generally. Our brains are built to think—thoughts are their natural product—and you will find that your brain goes on producing all kinds of thoughts even as you are meditating and trying to focus your attention on other things. What mindfulness meditation does for us is begin to change our relationship to the thoughts occurring, especially as we gradually learn to consider them as sensory input rather than facts or events we need to respond to. Thoughts provide important information, but they are not fundamentally different from or more important than, say, the taste of a pear or hearing a Mozart symphony. This can be a difficult lesson to learn because

> *"In attention there is no focusing, no choice; there is complete awareness without any interpretation."*
>
> Jiddu Krishnamurti, from his book *As One Is*

thoughts present themselves as reflections of reality. In other words, they present themselves as true. But just because you think something doesn't mean it's true, or even particularly important.

Let's consider an example of the tricky ways thoughts can make us believe things that aren't necessarily true. Imagine you send a text to a friend, inviting him to your birthday dinner. Hours later, you still haven't heard back, even though this friend usually responds right away. By the time you go to bed that night, you've decided that he doesn't want to come and is trying to think of a good excuse; your feelings are hurt. Then the next day, you wake up to a text from him: "Sorry for the delay. Phone died, was out all day w/o my charger. I'd love to come!"

Just because you think something doesn't mean it's true.

Mindfulness practice can teach us about the nature of thinking, and perhaps even more importantly, it can teach us that *we are not our thoughts*. This might seem like an obvious or even silly point to make, but consider for a moment the negative thoughts you have about yourself—about your weight, your intelligence, or your career success. If you're like most of us, you probably have a set of negative thoughts about yourself that you've been thinking for years and which you find yourself returning to regularly. In her book *Says Who?*, mindfulness teacher Ora Nadrich explains how our thoughts can hold us captive and how using mindfulness can help reframe our attitude toward negative and fear-based thoughts, mindfully replacing them with productive, supportive thoughts.

We often allow—and rarely question the validity of—certain negative thoughts (for example, "I need to lose ten pounds," "I'm not talented enough to make VP," or "My spouse is too good for me"). If you've been thinking negative thoughts for long enough, you have probably come to believe in and identify with them. You think you *are* overweight or not good enough instead of recognizing that these are simply thoughts that you have about yourself that may not even be objectively accurate.

You are not your thoughts; you are the *thinker* of the thoughts. We could never act on *all* of our thoughts, and there are many thoughts we shouldn't act on or believe in if we want to live a healthy, well-balanced life. So, this mindfulness meditation practice will help you discern *which* thoughts support your goals and well-being and which thoughts are destructive or unhealthy and should be discarded.

In a mindfulness meditation, you practice checking in with all of the sensations and thoughts you are experiencing, as you experience them. Gradually, you will practice opening your awareness to the *simultaneous observation* of the various aspects of the moment—without any expectation, without any judgment, allowing them to fluidly change. The key to getting the most out of an Open Awareness Meditation is to allow everything to be *as it already is*. It is in our nature to want to change or improve things, especially if there is discomfort on any level. To the extent possible, you should try not to do that during your meditation practice and simply allow things to be as they are.

For example, you decide to meditate outdoors because it's a peaceful, quiet day with comfortable weather. As your meditation begins, you hear a car drive by, your neighbor's dog barking, and the gentle breeze of the wind. The mental perspective to hold here is that you accept and allow the dog to bark and the car to drive by, without entertaining the desire for things to be any different than they are. The thought may arise "Will that dog be quiet?" but your practice will be to let yourself have that thought without following it or dwelling on it. The sound of the car and the barking of the dog need not interrupt the meditation; rather, they can become a part of it. Of course, you should always try to meditate in a place where you will be safe and as undisturbed as possible, but keep in mind that in any meditation practice, a crucial component is to allow—even welcome—changes to the outside environment without interrupting the meditation. Simply observe, experience, and allow things to be as they are.

This Open Awareness Meditation will make you more aware of the thoughts passing through your mind. Studies show that the average individual thinks anywhere from 30,000 to 70,000 thoughts every single day. By holding an open-focus awareness, you create a larger mental "container" for your thoughts to pass through. Gradually, with regular practice, mindfulness will give you the opportunity to more clearly see and experience the many layers of your thinking process.

What You'll Get Out of It

On Day 1 you practiced focusing concentration on a particular thing: the breath. Today you will open your awareness to include the fullness of the moment you are in. We can compare our attention to light: If we focus our concentration on something, we might say that we are "shining a spotlight" on it. When we practice **open awareness**, rather than shining a spotlight on one particular thing, we might say that we allow our awareness to "shine" in all directions around us, like the glow of a candle flame. We will refer to this "glow" of awareness around us as our **field of awareness**.

Your field of awareness is the sum total of all of your sensory input. The practice of open awareness is an exercise in allowing your senses to experience the fullness of the present moment, becoming aware even of the subtleties that you may normally overlook, ignore, or miss altogether, like the temperature of the air around you or the faint creaking of floorboards. When we simply notice and *allow* things to be as they are, we naturally disengage from the impulses that would try to control or change things. This is not a practice in passivity or ignorance—quite the opposite. This is a practice in opening your mind and allowing yourself to receive all the information you possibly can before making any moves or taking any action. Notice the word *allow*. We do not force ourselves to pick up on sensory input; the awareness expands naturally from a practice of calm, relaxed *allowing*.

When we are *resistant* to something that is happening, we have a biological tendency to "brace for impact," which means we withdraw and tighten the muscles in our body. The mind then immediately begins thinking of all the way things could or should be different than they are.

When we are *open* to something, we tend to be more curious about, and even more willing to embrace, the unknown, which leaves the body more at ease. This allows us to be more open to understanding and learning about what we are experiencing. With an open mind, we tend to see more possibilities and multiple perspectives on things.

Open Awareness Meditation will strengthen your ability to really see things as they are and accept them for what they are.

By practicing Open Awareness Meditation, you will cultivate:

Discernment Open Awareness Meditation allows us to understand more about the moment we are in. The more we know in any circumstance, the more informed our decisions can be. Through practicing mindful awareness, we cultivate discernment by being more sensitive to the bigger picture and how the present moment relates to it. This increased understanding allows us to discern which thoughts we want to entertain, which thoughts we need to release, and what might be the right decision for us to make given the circumstances.

Decreased depression and increased happiness In studies published by *Scientific American*, *Science Daily*, and more, mindfulness meditation practices have been successfully applied as a treatment for depression and proven to ameliorate depression symptoms such as lethargy and lack of quality sleep. Other studies show increased happiness and joy. There are also reports of increased laughter after going through mindfulness training.

Core creativity In Dr. Ronald Alexander's book *Wise Mind, Open Mind*, he maps out the different ways that a mindfulness meditation practice can help you tap into your core creativity and the mental perspective of limitless possibilities.

Self-awareness and better decision-making We all have many sides to our personalities. As you practice observing your thoughts, you will become more aware of the tone of your internal voice and the kinds of thoughts you are having and develop the ability to intervene before saying or doing something you might regret.

Reduced stress Mindfulness practices are proven to have significant effects on reducing the physical symptoms of stress. It is well known throughout the medical community that stress aggravates just about every single health problem and illness. By reducing the symptoms of stress (like tension in the muscles and concentrated amounts of stress hormones in the blood stream), we reduce their negative effect on our overall health.

Perspective By developing awareness of the various aspects of your environment through Open Awareness Meditation, that same skill naturally transitions into other areas of your life, providing a sense of proportion, big-picture perspective, and being present within a larger context.

Improvement in your life Through the practice of witnessing things as they are, you will become more aware of your ability to change things that are not working for you. By becoming more attentive and aware of the thoughts arising in your mind, you will create the opportunity to question and reframe them.

What You'll Need

Today you will need:

- a comfortable chair or cushion where you can sit with your spine comfortably erect

- a quiet place to sit where you won't be easily disturbed (by someone walking in on you, for example)

- a timer (if you decide to use the timer on your smartphone, it is best to put the phone on airplane mode or silent to prevent distractions from incoming alerts)

- your Meditation Notebook and a pen or pencil

Get Started

Please read through this entire meditation before beginning. Ideally you will remember the instructions and not have to interrupt the meditation to check the next step.

For today's meditation you should be sitting up—or even standing. Try to have your weight comfortably balanced between your left and right sides. If you are sitting, I recommend allowing your hands to rest comfortably in your lap or on your knees rather than using one of the mudras introduced yesterday. If you choose to stand, have your arms resting comfortably at your sides.

On Day 1, the key points for posture were:

1. Sit comfortably.
2. Not so comfortably that you'll fall asleep.

Today, we add a third point:

3. Sit or stand with your back comfortably erect.

I attended a lecture by Harvard Medical School professor of psychology and Buddhist scholar Daniel P. Brown in which he explained that the popular notion of meditation solely as a relaxation technique is inaccurate and actually detrimental to the powerful mind-training effects of meditation. In a state of deep relaxation, the mind tends to wander. Sitting up straight or standing with an erect spine will support your mental alertness, making for an effective meditation.

As you sit, you will notice microchanges in the body. These can be any number of things, such as tension rising in your shoulders as you hear an unpleasant sound, subtle changes in the breath as you settle deeper into a relaxed state, or chills on your skin as the temperature in the room changes. The exercise is to practice holding a *soft focus*, open to experiencing all of these things at once.

Please read through this entire meditation before beginning. Ideally you will remember the instructions and not have to interrupt the meditation to check the next step.

OPEN AWARENESS MEDITATION

1. Find a place to sit or stand where you won't be disturbed.

2. Take a moment to get into a comfortable position that you will be able to maintain for the duration of the practice with as little movement or adjustment as possible.

3. Set your intention: "I will meditate for five minutes, opening my awareness to the various sounds, sensations, thoughts, and emotions that may arise and allowing everything to be as it is, just for these five minutes."

BEGIN MEDITATING

1. Set your timer for five minutes.

2. Allow your eyes to gently close.

3. Feel your breath as your lungs expand and contract.

4. Notice the sensations along the surface of your skin, feeling the air in the room.

5. Bring your awareness to the space above your head, noticing any sounds or movement in the space above you.

6. Move your awareness to the space below you, noticing where your body touches the cushion or floor. Notice any subtle vibrations from the floor.

7. Keeping your body in a restful stillness, bring your awareness to the space in front of you, as far as your senses can reach.

8. Next, notice any sounds or movement to your right.

9. Move your awareness to the space behind you, filling the room, even expanding beyond the room. (Any sounds on the other side of the walls?)

10. Move your awareness to your left.

11. Envision your awareness as a glow in all directions around you, mentally scanning all directions at once—simply witnessing the moment as it is.

12. If the mind wanders, bring your awareness back to the breath as it expands and contracts, and expand your awareness in all directions around you from there.

Wrap Up

It is always recommended to end a meditation gently and mindfully. For some people, this means slowly beginning to move and stretch the body before opening their eyes; for others, this means saying a brief prayer or setting an intention for their day, such as "And now, I am going to have an efficient, effective, positive workday." Whatever way is most natural for you to wrap up, go for it. What matters is that you give yourself a moment to exit the meditation without a sense of rushing. Transitioning mindfully out of meditation helps you keep the relaxed state developed during your practice, thus extending the "shelf life" of the benefits of calmness, clarity, and openness.

Take a moment to record the details of your meditation in the space provided at the end of the chapter. If you end up meditating for longer than the suggested five minutes, please be sure to note this.

If you have time, take a few minutes to write down your answers to the following in your Meditation Notebook:

- Did any particular thoughts or memories come to mind that stood out?

- Were there any sensations that surprised you? A sound or feeling that was unexpected?

- How did your experience with Open Awareness Meditation compare to your experience yesterday, with the Zazen Breath Awareness Meditation?

Go Deeper

10-minute meditation—or longer

Begin with the above meditation, but set your timer for 10 minutes instead of five. If after 10 minutes you feel you want to keep going, continue the meditation for as long as you wish. I typically recommend 20 to 40 minutes for a regular practice.

Go deeper throughout your day: mindful check-in

Do a mindful check-in at work—Take a brief moment to mindfully experience the workplace from your usual spot. Mentally scan in all directions around you.

Do a mindful check-in during your meals—Notice the fragrances, the sounds, and the thoughts arising in your mind.

Do a mindful check-in at the market—When visiting one of the places you usually do your shopping, take a moment to notice the temperature, the smells, the music, and the conversations happening in the background.

Anywhere you find yourself, do a mindful check-in—Whenever appropriate, take a moment to close your eyes and listen in all directions around you. Be present with wherever you are, whenever you are actually there. Take it all in!

Journal your experience:

- Where did you practice your mindful check-ins?

- Did you notice any sounds, fragrances, or anything else you may have missed before?

- What kinds of thoughts came up?

Recommended Reading

Satipatthana Sutta Discourses by S. N. Goenka

Says Who? by Ora Nadrich

Wise Mind, Open Mind by Dr. Ronald Alexander

As One Is by Jiddu Krishnamurti

Pointing Out the Great Way by Daniel P. Brown, PhD

NOTES: DAY 2

Date: ....   Time: ....

Length of meditation: ....

Posture: ....

Mudra used (if applicable): ....

In a few words (e.g., easy, challenging, relaxing, boring) describe how you found the meditation:

....

....

....

....

Mindful Observation

MEDITATION LENGTH: 10 MINUTES

What Is It?

Mindful observation is an open-eye meditation in which you gently lock your gaze on an everyday object without moving your eyes. It is both a practice in stillness and in seeing something as if for the first time (similar to beginner's mind). In an ancient yogic eye-gazing practice called **trataka**, it is emphasized that your gaze on the object of observation should be direct and intentional but not strained or forced. You're not *concentrating* or doing anything that requires effort—you're gently resting your awareness on the object you've chosen to mindfully observe.

On Day 1, you practiced focusing your attention on a single, specific aspect of what you were experiencing in the moment—your breath. You'll use that skill again today, but instead of focusing on your breath, you'll focus on something external—an everyday object of your choice. In today's practice, you keep your eyes open.

On Day 2, you opened your mind to seeing the bigger picture. For today's meditation, you'll use that same skill to look with fresh eyes at an everyday object. Whether it's something as complex as a cell phone or computer, or an item as simple as a candle or spoon, all of these things had to be designed, developed, built, and transported, and all of the necessary materials had to be sourced, refined, and used to build

TRATAKA

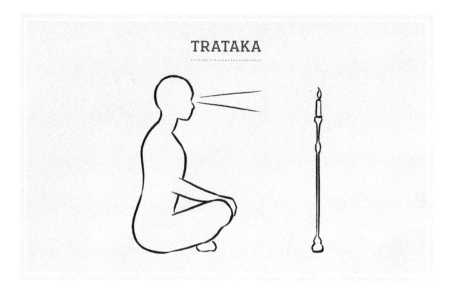

the seemingly mundane objects that surround us every day. Today's practice is to build awareness that there is more to what you are gazing at than initially meets the eye.

Through the practice of mindful observation, you will become more aware of what you're actually looking at. This practice is not simply a study of an object; it's exercising your capacity to take the time to look closely, with a relaxed approach, at something in front of you. This helps develop the curious and inquisitive nature of the mind. In *The Yoga Sutras of Patanjali*, it is said that developing this kind of relaxed, focused attention enhances the advanced mind power to understand and process universal wisdom far beyond what the untrained mind could comprehend.

For the exercise today, you will sit in a comfortable position with open eyes, gently observing the object of meditation. You won't be picking up or touching the object, just simply allowing your gaze to rest upon it.

In the meditation on Day 1, when your attention wandered from the breath, you noticed the wandering and brought your awareness back to the breath. Today you will follow a similar model for this Mindful Observation Meditation. You will gaze directly at the object, and when your eyes wander away from it, you will gently guide your gaze back to the object.

What You'll Get Out of It

Mindful observation holds the same mindful awareness as the open awareness exercise, but with open eyes gently directing attention to a specific object.

There are numerous cultures all over the world that practice various forms of open-eye meditation. Some require a constant gaze on a specific object, such as a candle, a **mandala** or **yantra** (kaleidoscopic artwork sacred in the Hindu faith, among other religions, symbolizing the unified universe), mystical words and sacred letters (as seen in Christianity and Kabbalah), and even gazing into the eyes of another person in an intimate "soul gazing" meditation (as practiced in both Indian Tantra and Hawaiian indigenous spiritual traditions).

Mindful observation generates many of the same benefits as other mindfulness practices, including self-awareness, reduced stress, and decreased symptoms of depression and anxiety. Clinical research on trataka (open-eye gazing meditation) is underway, and studies are being done to test the ancient claims of natural vision repair, improved memory, reduced anxiety, and positive effects on confidence and patience. Studies are also being done on the effects of which direction the eyes gaze during meditation.

By practicing Mindful Observation Meditation, you will cultivate:

Focus and concentration Developing the ability to focus intently without a sense of strain exercises the subtle ability to stay focused in other areas of life, such as work or when performing any task requiring sustained attention.

Willpower There is a silent act of will at play when we observe the impulse to allow our eyes to wander, then gently override it. This develops the mental fortitude and willpower to stick to whatever it is that we are focusing on or working with.

Stress reduction As with all exercises in training awareness, research has shown that as you focus your attention on a specific task, like gently gazing in one spot without moving your body, your conscious mind begins to disengage from other thoughts and concerns. This gives the mind and body a break from stressors and can reduce physical symptoms of stress like high blood pressure and difficulty sleeping.

Thought awareness As your gaze rests on your meditation object, your thoughts will continue to move through their natural rhythm. Mindful observation is a great technique for focusing the mind and cultivating awareness of the thoughts passing through your mind. You will notice that as the mind begins to wander, so do the eyes.

Gratitude By practicing mindful observation, you will become more aware of the virtues and qualities of what you are observing—a simple but useful spoon or a beautiful flower—which unlocks appreciation and gratitude for what you have. Cultivating a sense of gratitude in itself has been scientifically proven to have numerous health benefits. In an article for *Psychology Today*, psychotherapist Amy Morin, author of *13 Things Mentally Strong People Don't Do*, cited the scientific benefits of gratitude, such as improved physical and mental health, increased empathy, mental strength, self-esteem, and even better sleep.

What You'll Need

Today you will need:

* a comfortable chair or cushion where you can sit with your spine comfortably erect

- a quiet place to sit where you won't be easily disturbed (by someone walking in on you, for example)

- a timer (if you decide to use the timer on your smartphone, it is best to put the phone on airplane mode or silent to prevent distractions from incoming alerts)

- your Meditation Notebook and a pen or pencil

- a meditation object (see Get Started for suggestions)

Get Started

Begin by choosing your **meditation object**. It can have significance to you, if you like (maybe a crystal or a figurine), or it can simply be an everyday object, such as a jar, a candle, or a flower. In the traditional yogic trataka practice, there are extra-tall candlesticks designed for use in seated meditation (their height being tall enough for a candle to rest comfortably at eye level). For our purposes, any everyday object will do, although beautiful objects typically make the experience that much more enjoyable.

Now, set up your meditation space by finding a table, box, or dresser on which to place your meditation object. The goal is to not be looking either too far below or too far above your natural eye line. Once the object is at the right height, find a **gazing point**, a specific part of the object on which to rest your eyes so they aren't moving up and down and all around the object. You can also do this practice by hanging a small image, piece of art, or post-it on the wall at your seated eye level.

Please read through this entire meditation before beginning. Ideally you will remember the instructions and not have to interrupt the meditation to check the next step.

MINDFUL OBSERVATION

1. Find a place to sit where you won't be disturbed.

2. If you haven't already, set up your meditation space by finding a table, box, or dresser on which to place your meditation object. The goal is to not be looking either too far below or too far above your natural eye line.

3. Take a moment to get into a comfortable position that you will be able to maintain for the duration of the practice with as little movement or adjustment as possible. You should be able to rest your gaze comfortably forward at the meditation object.

4. Set your intention: "I will meditate for 10 minutes, effortlessly directing my attention at this object, allowing myself to see this object differently while resting in the stillness of my body and observing the thoughts arising in my mind. I will allow everything to be as it is, just for these 10 minutes."

BEGIN MEDITATING

1. Set your timer for 10 minutes.

2. Allow your eyes to rest comfortably on the object. Find your gazing point.

3. Take a few deep breaths to help release any tension in the body.

4. Allow the body to find relaxed stillness, and gently breathe through any impulse to shift or fidget.

5. Consider the object's size, color, and texture. Let its visual presence fill your awareness.

6. Look at the object with fresh eyes, as if you've never seen it before. If you were seeing it for the first time and didn't know what it was or where it came from, what would you think of it?

7. When your eyes wander away from the object, simply bring them back to your original gazing point. If your awareness wanders, bring it back to the breath, then gently back to the object.

Wrap Up

Mindfully transition out of your meditation by gently stretching your body and taking a few deep breaths. For an open-eye meditation, it is advisable to sit for a moment with your eyes closed at the end of the meditation. As I mentioned in Day 2, many people find it helpful to state an intention for the rest of their day, such as "And now, I am going to spend a day with my family, practicing patience, mindfulness, and gratitude." Whatever way is most natural for you to wrap up your practice, go for it. What matters is that you give yourself a moment to exit the meditation without a sense of rushing. Transitioning mindfully out of meditation helps you keep the relaxed state developed during your practice, thus extending the "shelf life" of the benefits of calmness, clarity, and openness.

Take a moment to record the details of your meditation in the space provided at the end of the chapter.

If you have time, take a few minutes to write down your answers to the following in your Meditation Notebook:

- What object did you choose?

- What were its most noticeable features?

- Did you find it challenging or easy to maintain your gaze on your gazing point?

- How did your open-eye meditation experience compare to the two closed-eye practices from Day 1 and Day 2?

Go Deeper

Meditation on a loved one

Select an image of a friend, a family member, or another loved one. Use the same meditation as above, resting your gaze on the eyes of this person. Journal your experience in your Meditation Notebook. What thoughts came up? What memories stand out?

Mirror-Gazing Meditation

Sit or stand in front of a mirror and set your timer for 5 to 10 minutes. Follow the Mindful Observation Meditation instructions, gazing directly into your own eyes. Journal your experience. What kinds of thoughts came to mind? Did you notice anything different about yourself or the thoughts that arose in your mind about yourself?

Go deeper throughout your day:
There is so much more to know!

Because we could never go into a deep mindful observation on everything we see, this exercise helps us gradually open our minds to the realization that there is so much more to know about everything. Whenever the idea comes to mind throughout the day, notice the many things in your environment. Silently repeat this phrase to yourself: "There is so much more to know about ____" Complete the sentence with whatever it is you happen to see. This shouldn't feel forced or strained. Simply glance around, noticing what your gaze rests on, and silently acknowledge that "there is so much more to know."

For example:

- There is so much more to know about that chair.
- There is so much more to know about that door.
- There is so much more to know about that person.

Throughout your day, allow this practice to open your mind to seeing things differently by recognizing that there is so much more to know about the people, places, and things you are surrounded by.

Recommended Reading

The Yoga Sutras of Patanjali by Sri Swami Satchidananda

A Course in Miracles by The Foundation for Inner Peace

The Golden Ratio by Mario Livio

Break the Norms by Chandresh Bhardwaj

Fundamentals of Hawaiian Mysticism by Charlotte Berney

NOTES: DAY 3

Date: .... Time: ....

Length of meditation: ....

Posture: ....

Mudra used (if applicable): ....

In a few words (e.g., easy, challenging, relaxing, boring) describe how you found the meditation:

....

....

....

....

....

....

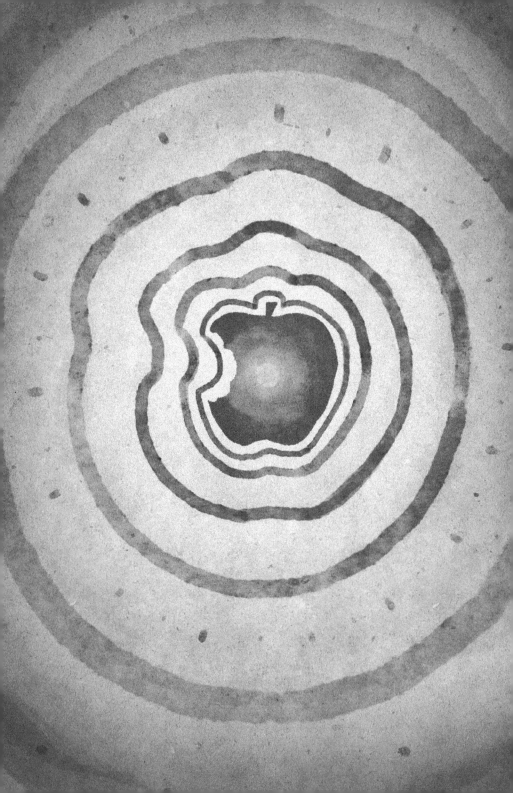

Mindful Eating

MEDITATION LENGTH: 10 MINUTES

What Is It?

Mindful eating is a form of meditation in which you slow down the process of eating, allowing yourself to experience it fully. Eating is something we engage in many times a day, usually in a pretty "mindless" way. By that I mean it's very common for people to be distracted while eating because they're also watching TV, listening to music, socializing, checking e-mails, texting, or using social media.

Sometimes we eat so mindlessly that eating itself *is* the distraction from our main task—like when we eat while driving. In studies published by The National Highway Traffic Safety Administration, it was found that an estimated 80 percent of car accidents were the result of eating while driving, and about 65 percent of "close calls," or almost-accidents, were also caused by drivers distracted by eating or drinking.

Mindful eating doesn't just mean chewing more slowly or taking smaller bites; it also encompasses *when, how,* and *what* we eat. Mindful eating helps you focus on the details of the in-the-moment experience of seeing, smelling, touching, and tasting your food.

Mindful eating is about appreciating what it is that you're eating, and it requires the same kind of concentration that was introduced in Day 1. For today's meditation practice, you are going to apply that focus to the entire process and experience of what you're eating.

As we learned on Day 2, you can turn any activity into a meditation practice simply by turning your mindful attention toward it. Eating is a great activity to practice mindfully because it's a rich and complex sensory experience that most of us do on autopilot; paying attention to eating opens up a whole new world. On Day 3, we looked with open eyes intently at a meditation object. Mindful eating begins with the sense of sight—taking a good look at the color, texture, and portion size of what you're about to eat.

Most of the time, the amount of food on our plate is rarely related to what our body's nutritional needs actually are. When we eat something strictly for pleasure, not for the purpose of satisfying genuine hunger or meeting nutritional needs, mindful eating can help us experience that pleasure in deeper, more gratifying ways.

For example, my mother is a gourmet chocolatier. When she was preparing to open her business, she tested out new recipes for caramels and chocolate truffles. She always gave my dad, my brothers, and me the "rejects," which we happily ate. When a recipe experiment was complete, my mom would cut the chocolate truffle in half. She would then look closely at the color and texture of the chocolate shell and the truffle's filling. Next, she would take a small bite, close her eyes, and mindfully examine the texture with her tongue. Sometimes she might taste test a recipe a few times, saying the texture was "too grainy" or that the filling was "too sour" before getting it right. For the most part, my brothers and I would just scarf down whatever she gave us, but her mindful, well-trained palate picked up on subtleties that the rest of us missed. She uses mindful eating practices to adjust recipes, experiment with new ingredients, and develop increasingly better products.

What You'll Get Out of It

When a new meditation studio, The DEN Meditation, opened near where I live in Los Angeles, I was approached to host a Mindful Wine Tasting workshop, and I happily accepted. In conducting these tastings, I've found that when people really take the time to learn about the wine they are drinking and experience and enjoy every sip, they tend to drink less. Some people also found that they were more sensitive to the effects of the alcohol. One participant shared that she typically has two glasses of wine with dinner but felt satisfied during our Mindful Wine Tasting after just one-third of one glass!

In other words, by practicing mindful eating (and mindful drinking!), you will cultivate:

Awareness of how much you need to eat In a study published by *The American Journal of Clinical Nutrition*, eating attentively was discovered to make people eat less. Those who were eating while distracted or entertained tended to eat more at that meal.

Awareness of why you are eating When practicing mindfulness as it relates to eating, you will better notice your thoughts and feelings about eating. It is common for people today to "eat our feelings," to numb ourselves from unwelcome feelings by eating when we aren't physically hungry.

Greater meal satisfaction It is common for people who begin eating mindfully to enjoy their meals more, find them more satisfying, and even remember more about them.

Better diet-related health Fast, inattentive eating has been linked to excessive weight gain and even the development of type 2 diabetes.

Increased mindful attention skills Mindful eating supports the development of all the skills cultivated in mindfulness practices: attention, present-moment awareness, and recognition of and mastery over the wandering mind.

Better eating choices When we eat out of habit, we don't have any control over what or how we are eating—in fact, that is the very nature of habit. Habit exists to help automate behaviors, which causes the behavior to become more efficient. However, automation also means no choice. When we eat mindfully, we may become aware of the impulse to return to automatic behaviors, but our awareness helps us override those impulses and make healthier (and safer) eating-related decisions.

Improved digestion and nutrient absorption Thorough chewing and slower eating makes it much easier for your body to process and digest meals. It is also said that eating with your hands (touching your food directly rather than using a fork or other utensil) sends signals throughout your body about what you are eating, allowing your stomach to ready itself for what it will receive, which also aids in digestion.

What You'll Need

For today's meditation, as with all meditation techniques, you don't need much to get you going. Whether you sit on the floor or a chair is up to you and often depends on where you decide to practice—home, work, etc. Each day may be different as well, depending on how you're feeling that day. Today you will need:

- a comfortable chair at a table where you can sit with your spine comfortably erect

- a quiet place to sit where you won't be easily disturbed (by someone walking in on you, for example)

- a timer (if you decide to use the timer on your smartphone, it is best to put the phone on airplane mode or silent to prevent distractions from incoming alerts)

- your Meditation Notebook and a pen or pencil

- an apple, banana, or other simple fruit

Get Started

Please read through this entire meditation before beginning. Ideally you will remember the instructions and not have to interrupt the meditation to check the next step.

MINDFUL EATING

BEFORE MEDITATING

1. If you live with others, try to plan a time when you won't be disturbed or distracted.

2. Find a table to sit at with your fruit. Clear everything else from the table besides your one piece of fruit. Feel free to lay out a placemat and plate or napkin, if you'd like.

3. Take a moment to get comfortable so all of your attention can be focused on what you are about to eat.

4. Set your intention: "I will mindfully eat this fruit for 10 minutes as a form of meditation, to enjoy, appreciate, and assimilate this food more completely."

BEGIN MEDITATING

1. Set your timer for 10 minutes.

2. Sit with the fruit on the table in front of you. Do not pick it up right away.

3. Take it in visually: its size, color, shape, details.

4. After a few moments of observing the fruit, pick it up.

5. Slowly touch the different parts of the fruit, noticing all the many details of this particular fruit, like its texture, weight, and temperature.

6.   Take a few gentle deep breaths through your nose. Can you smell the fruit just holding it in your hand? What does it smell like? Sweet? Musty? Something else?

7.   Now, lift the fruit gently toward your nose, close your eyes, and smell the fruit up close. Notice the qualities of the fruit, the thoughts that come to mind, and possibly even the watering in your mouth. Take your time. Don't rush.

8.   Open your eyes and take a bite, making your bite about half the size you would normally take. Close your eyes again.

9.   Before chewing, feel the piece of fruit in your mouth.

10.   Chew slowly. Notice the various textures.

11.   Notice the various tastes. Do they change as you chew?

12.   Notice the changes with every chew. Keep your eyes closed to focus your attention within your mouth.

13.   Swallow the piece of fruit. Mentally follow the bite as it moves down your throat and into your stomach. Notice where you feel it.

14.   Slowly continue to eat the fruit, one mindful bite at a time. If your mind wanders away from the experience of eating, gently bring your focus back to your mindful eating practice.

Wrap Up

End your meditation slowly and mindfully. Consider taking a moment to set an intention for the day, such as, "Today, I am going to be more mindfully aware of what I eat and drink." Give yourself a moment to exit the meditation without a sense of rushing. Transitioning mindfully out of meditation helps you keep the relaxed state developed during your practice, thus extending the "shelf life" of the benefits of calmness, clarity, and openness.

When your timer goes off, check in with your body. Did you finish eating the fruit or is there still some left? Make notes about your experience in the space provided at the end of the chapter or in your Meditation Notebook.

- What did you notice about the fruit before you ate it?

- Did it seem fragrant or mild?

- What did you notice while you were eating it?

- Did you feel the impulse to eat quickly?

- Were you able to feel comfortable savoring each bite, or did you find yourself in need of additional stimulation, like music or TV?

As you slowly make the transition to the rest of your day, notice how you feel after eating the fruit. Too often we eat foods that taste good but don't actually meet our nutritional needs. This can leave us feeling lethargic and bloated and sometimes even dehydrated or irritable. Eating foods that are fresh and nutritionally dense, like fruits, can provide the body the fuel it needs to function optimally, giving us a boost of energy and a sense of wellness.

Go Deeper

Make a mealtime ritual

- Set aside time for at least one meal a day to be eaten at home.

- Clean off the table and set a place for yourself and anyone else who will be joining you.

- Turn off the TV and all electronic devices that could interrupt.

- You can light candles, put flowers on the table, anything to make the moment special.

- Before you begin to eat, take a few moments to appreciate your meal and anyone who may be with you. You may want to close your eyes and say a brief blessing over the food.

- Enjoy your meal mindfully, following the meditation instructions above.

- If you have friends or family with you, engage in mindful conversation about the textures and flavors of the meal.

Try some new recipes

Meditation coach and chef Cassandra Bodzak offers recipes paired with specially designed meditations in her cookbook *Eat With Intention*, which places a strong emphasis on mindful eating. Try these or other mindfulness-oriented recipes to be more present during your meals.

Put the fork down between each bite

Slow down your eating process. Take a few breaths between each bite, swallowing and putting the fork down before continuing to eat.

Pay attention

Pay attention to what you are eating. Read the ingredients, look at the food itself, and tune in to your body's nutritional needs.

Go deeper throughout your day: Be a mindful eater

- To prevent unhealthy snacking, stop by a health food store and pick up a few organic fruits that can be easily eaten, such as bananas, apples, or pears.

- Write down everything you eat. You're not counting calories, just making note of what you eat. Do this for a few days and notice the nutrients you are or are not taking in. Keep track of your feelings, thoughts, and emotions that arise before, after, and during your meals.

Recommended Reading

Savor: Mindful Eating, Mindful Life by Thich Nhat Hanh and Lilian Cheung

A Course in Weight Loss by Marianne Williamson

Mindful Eating by Jan Chozen Bays

Eat With Intention by Cassandra Bodzak

Eat What You Love, Love What You Eat by Michelle May

NOTES: DAY 4

Date: ....   Time: ....

Length of meditation: ....

In a few words (e.g., easy, challenging, relaxing, boring), describe how you found this meditation:

....

....

....

....

....

....

Observing Your Emotions

MEDITATION LENGTH: 10 MINUTES

What Is It?

Your basic task in this meditation is to notice and acknowledge your emotions as they arise without doing anything else about them. You do this meditation seated and with your eyes closed, turning your awareness to the breath, as on Day 1, then opening your awareness throughout the body, similar to the Open Awareness Meditation on Day 2. You observe your emotions, your thoughts, and your physical sensations. They are all closely related, and different emotions will trigger different physiological responses. In the simplest terms, "positive" emotions make you feel "good" and "negative" emotions make you feel "bad." Emotions are transient—they come and go like waves in the ocean—but they have a powerful influence. This is important to realize, and mindful monitoring of your emotions will sensitize you to them and the impact they have on you from moment to moment. Gradually, with practice, you will become more and more adept at mindfully living *alongside* them rather than allowing them to dictate your behavior.

In this practice, you allow yourself to experience whatever emotion arises: no judging, storytelling, or explaining, just mindfully experiencing whatever comes up. This can be surprisingly challenging, especially if **repressed emotions** make themselves known. We are typically discouraged from expressing unpleasant emotions, and sometimes we are too unaware of our emotions to ever learn how to express them in a healthy way. But repressing or ignoring unpleasant emotions doesn't make them go away—all it does is increase the likelihood that they will show up later, in a counterproductive way.

Still, we often try to use pleasurable things at our immediate disposal to numb and distract ourselves from painful emotions. Any activity done in excess—eating, drinking, sex, shopping, social media use—can act as a **numbing agent**, "protecting" us from the uncomfortable experience of negative emotions. In reality, these numbing agents are not protecting us from the negative emotions but rather helping us repress and avoid them.

Whenever we're in a state of heightened emotion, whether it's a positive emotion (such as excitement or euphoric happiness) or a negative emotion (such as anger or intense frustration), we tend to make poor decisions that we regret later on, or say and do things we don't mean. Heightened emotional states, while sometimes uncomfortable, are therefore excellent times to practice mindfulness. In becoming deeply aware of our emotions, the thoughts that surround them (the self-talk), and the physical sensations that come with them, we develop the capacity to self-regulate. In other words, we develop the ability to soothe ourselves and bring ourselves down from an uncomfortable level of emotional intensity.

There are even times when we are "caught up" in someone else's emotions, and mindful observation of these emotions can help determine if what you are feeling belongs to you or if it is the result of someone else's emotional expression. This is an important skill for anyone who is highly sensitive to the emotions of others (an **empath**). Most people are sensitive to the emotions of others to some degree, but managing an acute sensitivity can be challenging, especially for those unaware that they are experiencing the emotions of someone else. Observing your emotions is a powerful tool in recognizing what exactly you are feeling and what you can do to improve or calm your emotional response.

That same aware-but-not-attached mind-set you began practicing with sounds and thoughts on Day 2, you will now begin applying toward your emotions, noting information from sensory input. For example, as the emotion arises, observe it objectively by using mental noting: "Wow, I'm feeling really frustrated right now," or "I'm feeling impatient." Then notice any sensations in the body: "My shoulders feel tight," or "My breathing has gotten shorter and faster."

Eventually, you will also begin to notice the thoughts that surround the emotion. As all of this information—the feelings, the sensations, and the thoughts around them—comes together, you will gain new insight about your present emotional state, giving you the power to self-regulate.

What You'll Get Out of It

There are subtle but powerful benefits to understanding your emotions and emotional patterns. By practicing observing your emotions, you will cultivate:

Appreciation of the good times Time flies when you're having fun, but challenging experiences seem to have the opposite effect. When you are experiencing a positive emotion, such as love, happiness, or gratitude, mindful observation of your feelings can help you savor the moment, as you did on Day 4 with mindful eating. Rather than savoring the taste of a delicious meal, you will savor the experience of a beautiful emotional state.

Stress management skills Typically, in a heightened emotional state, it is very hard to objectively see the different dynamics and aspects of any given circumstance, which can cause us to place blame or shame somewhere it does not belong. Through practicing mindful observation of your emotions, you will begin to notice that the emotions you feel are actually *separate from* the stories you tell yourself about why you're feeling them. This is an important distinction for stress management. When under emotional pressure, we rarely express a sense of calm confidence, which is our most balanced and rational state.

Self-acceptance and acceptance of others Evaluating your emotions objectively gives you the opportunity to become more aware of your own emotional habits without forcing them to be anything other than what they actually are. This practice cultivates self-acceptance, or allowing yourself to feel the way you do. As you become more aware of the subtleties of your own emotional self, you will become naturally more open and forgiving of others and their need to express what they're feeling, too.

The ability to release mental baggage A grudge is an underlying anger, prejudice, or dislike that is held on to and not released. Bitterness and negativity without a healthy release can cause excess emotional baggage, putting a strain on emotional health. When we are able to let go of our grudges and judgment of others, we are released from the psychological weight of that judgment. This doesn't mean condoning or endorsing negative behaviors, but it does release us from the mental attachment to the associated pain and negativity. This lightens our load and keeps us open to new experiences and possibilities.

Improved emotional self-regulation Conveying **emotional self-regulation** means being able to express your emotions in a way that is healthy and respectful of those around you. It is perfectly normal to have the occasional emotional overreaction. When this happens, mindful observation of your emotions will help you separate the temporary experience of the emotion from the reality of the bigger picture. Every circumstance is unique, and practicing mindfulness can bring your awareness to the present moment so that your words and actions can best reflect the needs of the moment and what's actually happening around you.

The ability to identify your needs When children cry, it is often because they are unable to articulate exactly what it is that they need. They expect an adult within earshot to be able to identify their imminent needs and meet them. As adults, we can sometimes feel emotional without immediately knowing what it is we're feeling and why we are feeling it. Through a mindful observation of the emotion and the associated thoughts and sensations, you will better understand what exactly you need in order to have your needs met.

Equanimity and emotional balance There are inevitable challenges in life, and there is no denying that. The practice of mindful emotional awareness helps the mind develop a sense of that "bigger picture" mentioned on Day 2. The more you are able to adjust your perspective from being "inside" the emotion to being "alongside" it, the steadier your mind will be, which will help you make rational, healthy decisions.

What You'll Need

Today you will need:

- a comfortable chair or cushion where you can sit with your spine comfortably erect

- a quiet place to sit where you won't be easily disturbed (by someone walking in on you, for example)

- a timer (if you decide to use the timer on your smartphone, it is best to put the phone on airplane mode or silent to prevent distractions from incoming alerts)

- your Meditation Notebook and a pen or pencil

Get Started

Emotions are fleeting and can change in the blink of an eye. Receiving a text with bad news can interrupt even the most joyful moment and send us into an emotional downward spiral. The same is also true of moments of sadness and grief; a friend or loved one can inspire a smile or even a laugh when we're feeling sad or depleted. By tuning in to your direct experience, you can override the patterns of your mind that can jump to judgment, blame, and attack; you can also make clear, wise decisions even in the heat of passion.

When practicing a meditation relating to emotions, it is always advisable to take it slow and be gentle with yourself. The goal here is not to unearth deep trauma or seek out repressed emotions. Rather, this is a practice in tuning in to where you really are *right now*.

The aim is to witness your emotions *as they are*, without judgment, analysis, or explanation. This can be challenging, because when we experience a negative emotion or thought, the natural tendency is to find a solution or try to "fix" what is wrong. As you gently acknowledge your emotions and the thoughts arising in your mind, your subconscious will immediately begin to work on a solution. You will notice different thoughts, perhaps about a "solution" or perhaps about something else. The idea right now is to simply observe. Trust that your subconscious mind will be working at the solution while you're practicing mindful observation of your emotions.

Please read through this entire meditation before beginning. Ideally you will remember the instructions and not have to interrupt the meditation to check the next step.

OBSERVING YOUR EMOTIONS

1. Find a place to sit where you won't be disturbed.

2. Take a moment to get into a comfortable position that you will be able to maintain for the duration of the practice with as little movement or adjustment as possible.

3. Set your intention: "I will meditate for 10 minutes, opening my mind to observing my emotions, the thoughts that surround them, and the physical sensations that arise with them."

BEGIN MEDITATING

1. Set your timer for 10 minutes.

2. Allow your eyes to gently close. Or, if you prefer, allow your eyes to rest partially open, maintaining a soft, unfocused downward gaze—don't look *at* anything specific.

3. Settle in by shifting your attention to your breath for a few inhales and exhales.

4. You could start by noticing how you are feeling about meditating. Are you happy to be sitting? Hopeful? Curious? Bored?

5. Try not to go too deeply into an analysis of your emotional state, but hold an open awareness of it.

6. Once you have a good sense of your current emotion, notice any thoughts surrounding it.

7. Notice any particular sensations in the body.

8. Notice any impulses to move or adjust the body and breathe through them. Allow yourself to decompress, letting go of tension so that any physical sensations related to the emotion might become more apparent.

9. When the mind wanders, bring your awareness back to the breath, then to the emotions.

10. Don't worry how frequently your mind wanders; just return your attention to the breath, noticing its rhythm, and then to the emotions, the thoughts surrounding the emotions, and any physical sensations.

Wrap Up

If challenging emotions arose during the meditation, take a few deep breaths in and out through the nose, do some light stretching, and drink a glass of water to help regulate yourself. Then take a moment to record the details of your meditation in the space provided at the end of the chapter.

If you have time, take a few minutes to consider the following, and write about your experience in your Meditation Notebook. Keep in mind that you will be referring back to these journal entries, so in a way, they are notes to your future self.

* What emotion(s) did you experience?

* Do you have a prominent underlying emotion you seem to live with most days?

* What thoughts came up around that emotion?

* Did you feel it anywhere in particular in your body? Where?

* Did any particular individuals or circumstances come to mind?

Go Deeper

Happiness journaling

- Set your timer for 10 minutes.

- In your Meditation Notebook, write down all the things that make you feel happy (think Julie Andrews in *The Sound of Music*, and write out your "favorite things").

- Keep writing until the 10 minutes is up.

Go deeper throughout your day: gratitude affirmations

Throughout your day, whenever you feel comfortable, silently repeat the following gratitude affirmations:

- I am so happy and grateful for my many friends and loving relationships.

- I am so happy and grateful for my sense of self.

- I am so happy and grateful for my opportunities to learn and grow.

- I am so happy and grateful for ____.

Recommended Reading

Real Happiness by Sharon Salzberg

Meditation Secrets for Women by Camille Maurine and Lorin Roche, PhD

The Empath's Survival Guide by Judith Orloff, MD

Radical Acceptance by Tara Brach, PhD

Shift into Freedom by Loch Kelly, M.Div., LCSW

NOTES: DAY 5

Date: .... Time: ....

Length of meditation: ....

Posture: ....

Mudra used (if applicable): ....

In a few words (e.g., easy, challenging, relaxing, boring), describe how you found this meditation:

....

....

....

....

....

....

"Mindfulness is simply being aware of what is happening right now without wishing it were different; enjoying the pleasant without holding on when it changes (which it will); being with the unpleasant without fearing it will always be this way (which it won't)."

James Baraz

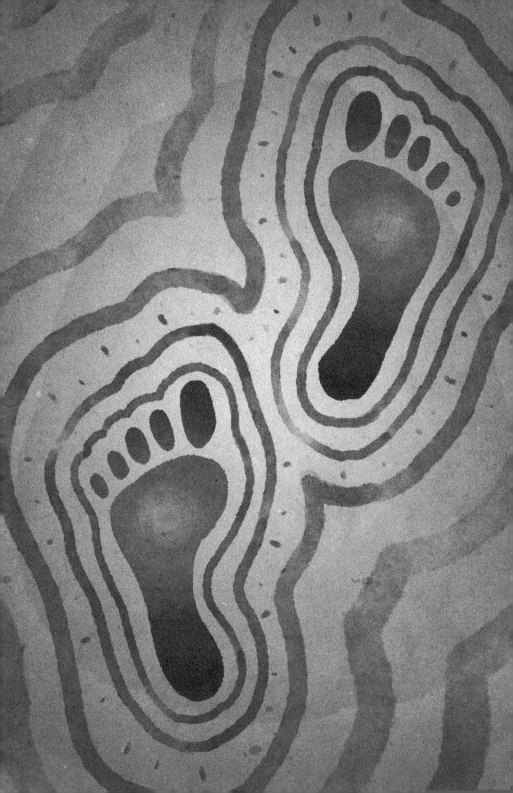

Walking Meditation

MEDITATION LENGTH: 10 MINUTES

What Is It?

Today you will practice a Walking Meditation, which is a form of **mindful walking** and one of the most basic forms of **moving meditation**. Unlike seated meditation, moving meditation requires more interaction between the mind and the body, and between the body and the external environment. For some people, movement of the body makes it easier to bring their awareness into that part of the body. Other examples of moving meditations include yoga, dance, and even sporting activities. For example, when highly trained athletes are competing, they have absolute awareness of their bodies and surroundings and precise command of their actions. Just as we learned how eating a piece of fruit can become a meditation if done mindfully, just about any activity can be turned into a meditation through mindful awareness.

In his book *After the Ecstasy, the Laundry*, Jack Kornfield shares the message that even though living a spiritual path can ignite powerful insights and experiences of spontaneous bliss, our day-to-day lives are always there waiting to be mindfully experienced, even such "unspiritual" tasks as doing the laundry.

Most of us are so used to doing things like walking, cleaning, and doing the laundry that we don't even think twice about it. A Walking Meditation consists of slowly, mindfully taking gentle steps and focusing your mental awareness on each step—and each aspect of each step. You bring your attention into the heel, ball, and toes of your feet, feeling each in turn as they press against the ground.

In many silent meditation retreats, mindful walking is practiced between periods of seated meditation. This is because the zazen meditation postures mentioned in Day 1 reduce or cut off blood circulation to the legs, and Walking Meditation can increase the blood flow throughout the body without breaking the meditative state cultivated in a seated meditation.

Walking Meditation begins by standing with your feet shoulder-width apart, back comfortably erect, hands resting clasped, and eyes holding a soft, low gaze. The meditator often paces slowly and repeatedly along a path. The purpose for walking along the same path rather than exploring new terrain or walking down new pathways is to bring the focus of the mind to the walking itself, with as little distraction as possible. When you walk down a new path or do not have a designated route, one part of your mind is distracted, determining which way to go next, subtly exploring with the imagination the different possibilities. Mind wandering is counterproductive to the mind-training aspects of meditation.

"Walk as if you are kissing the Earth with your feet."

Thich Nhat Hanh, from his book *Peace Is Every Step*

Walking mindfully down a short, familiar path breaks up the Walking Meditation with brief stops at the end of the short path. In those moments when you turn around to pace in the opposite direction, you have a natural opportunity to notice if the mind has wandered. For this reason, I recommend that you find a path that will give you the opportunity to stop and turn around at least twice during today's 10-minute practice.

What You'll Get Out of It

Walking Meditation is especially effective when combined with a seated meditation practice. It is rarely used as a stand-alone practice and is most often worked into a seated meditation routine. The main reason for this is that in a meditation practice that emphasizes physical stillness, what is called "body consciousness" (an established sense of fullness and connectedness to the environment) is gradually left behind, which can be much more challenging to achieve in an active physical state. Walking Meditation does, however, produce many of the same benefits as other mindfulness practices, like concentration, focus, reduced stress, and sustained attention. Other benefits you will cultivate include:

Dignity and confidence In a conversation I had with former Buddhist monk Alan Clements, he said, "Mindfulness should be the most dignified way of living." When we live from a place of present-moment awareness, our actions become more gentle, more respectful, and more dignified. Our attitude toward ourselves becomes less extreme and more balanced, and is expressed as a healthy sense of confidence and security.

Intentional living The Buddha is quoted as saying, "If you are facing the right direction, all you need to do is keep on walking." We often find ourselves unsure of what to do next, impatient, and longing for something more. It can be very challenging to live—and walk—mindfully. In mindful walking, the experience of walking itself is the intention; we aren't walking to *get* anywhere. In fact, you pace the same path multiple times. This can help develop a sense of intentional living, intentional movement, and deliberate action.

Personal responsibility It is said that "you alone must walk the path"—that is, the path of personal growth and development. By bringing your mindfulness practice into a moving meditation, such as

Walking Meditation, a natural sense of inner resourcefulness arises, which can inspire feelings of strength, confidence, and personal responsibility.

Increased concentration When practicing mindful walking, especially outdoors, there can sometimes be a great deal of distraction (for example, the sounds of traffic, nature, other people, or animals). This exercise in relaxed concentration, moving deliberately, gracefully, mindfully, increases your ability to concentrate without strain or tension.

Better moods Walking stimulates the production and release of hormones like endorphins and the neurotransmitter serotonin. These two brain chemicals are known to elevate mood, regulate appetite, and support healthy memory.

Mind-body connection Directing your awareness to specific parts of the body when in motion provides an empowering sense of immediate feedback, meaning that when your brain fires the signal to "lift your left foot," and your awareness focuses on your left foot, you get an immediate sense of connection, allowing you to embrace your body as it moves. Walking mindfully also gives you the opportunity to walk with perfect balance.

Deeper connection to nature and community Mindful walking, when practiced outdoors, is a great way to connect to the rhythm of nature. Sometimes called "nature medicine," spending time outdoors can be deeply healing. When practicing in your neighborhood, you will see and become familiar with your surroundings in a deeper way than if you had simply rushed by, distracted by things to do and people to see. You will begin to notice details about the path and its surroundings that you may have overlooked before. This can generate a deep sense of familiarity and home.

Awareness of your surroundings Mindful walking helps cultivate the awareness of the many different parts of your body, keeping you focused on where you're going and what you're doing. In a world where many people walk with their eyes looking down at their cell phones, your increased awareness in the present moment can help prevent accidents and run-ins.

What You'll Need

For today's meditation, as with all meditation techniques, you don't need much to get you going. Today you'll need:

- someplace peaceful to walk
  - A park or a running track are good outdoor options. Ideally there will be a path. It will help if the place is familiar so you won't be too distracted by what's around you. You won't be going far; in fact, you will walk the same path repeatedly, back and forth.
  - If you'd rather practice this exercise indoors (which is great, too), you'll need a hallway or large room where you can walk clear of obstructions. Please note that you will need to walk about 20 paces.

- a timer (if you decide to use the timer on your smartphone, it is best to put the phone on airplane mode or silent to prevent distractions from incoming alerts)

- your Meditation Notebook and a pen or pencil

Get Started

To prepare for today's Walking Meditation, it's good to take a few moments beforehand to remind yourself of the things you've learned so far. Recall on Day 2 when you learned the concept of yin and yang. Think about the yin component of meditation and the relaxed, open awareness of experiencing different aspects of sensory input simultaneously in the present moment. Then recall the directed concentration, focused and alert, of the yang component of meditation.

Take a moment to find that sense of open relaxation and alert presence in the body. I often recommend that students briefly practice Zazen Breath Awareness Meditation (as in Day 1) prior to beginning a movement meditation like mindful walking. Once you've taken a moment or two to release tension in the body, and become present and aware of the breath, you are ready to begin your Walking Meditation.

Please read through this entire meditation before beginning. Ideally you will remember the instructions and not have to interrupt the meditation to check the next step.

WALKING MEDITATION

1. Find the best location for you to practice your Walking Meditation. I recommend walking about 20 paces in one direction, so try to choose a path that allows for that.

2. Designate starting and stopping points on your path so this will not distract you during the actual practice.

3. Set your intention: "I will walk slowly and mindfully for 10 minutes as a form of meditation. I will bring my awareness into my body, noticing all of the movements and functions that operate as I walk, and bringing my awareness back to the experience of walking when my mind wanders."

BEGIN MEDITATING

1. Start your timer for 10 minutes.

2. Stand at the beginning of the path, bringing your awareness into your body as you stand up straight, your back comfortably erect. Balance your weight evenly on both feet.

3. Gently clasp your hands together at a comfortable length, and rest them together either in front of or behind your body.

4. Keep a somewhat-low gaze, looking at the ground a few meters ahead of you.

5. Take a few deep breaths before you begin to help release any tension in the body.

6. Notice the feeling of the ground beneath your feet.

7. Slowly lift your left foot and take one step forward, about half the length of a regular step, placing your foot down slowly and mindfully.

8. Feel the weight of your body slowly shift forward onto that left foot. Make sure your left foot is completely down before lifting your right foot.

9. This might feel a little awkward at first, but stick with it, noticing your reaction without judgment. If your mind is wandering, it could be helpful to silently say "Step-ping left" as you make your left step.

10. Slowly lift your right foot and take one small step forward, feeling the sensation of your right foot suspended in the air as it moves forward and presses down on the ground. Notice the sensation of your body weight shifting to your right foot as you say "Step-ping right."

11. Walk at a steady pace: mindful but not glacially slow.

12. Notice the sensations throughout your body—muscles firing in your thighs and movement in your hips and even along your spine and in your arms.

13. Continue in the same manner for 20 paces.

14. Once you get to the end of your path (or your 20 paces), stop briefly and slowly turn around.

15. Notice when your mind wanders to things like a tree, a crack in the sidewalk, or a rustling in the bushes. Feel free to pause your walking for a moment to mindfully take in whatever has caught your interest.

16. Bring your awareness back to your walking, and continue as above, turning again after 20 paces, until your timer goes off.

Wrap Up

When you finish your Walking Meditation, take a few deep breaths, look around, and take in your environment. When you're new to mindfulness exercises, the subtleness of the practices can sometimes be surprising. According to some studies, now that you have been practicing for six days, you should be experiencing some of the stress-reducing benefits of meditation.

Keep track of your meditation practice in the space provided at the end of the chapter.

If you have time, take a few minutes to write down your answers to the following in your Meditation Notebook:

- What path did you choose to walk down?

- Did you notice anything new about this path that caught your eye?

- What kinds of thoughts arose as you walked?

- Did you find it easy or challenging to walk mindfully?

- Did you notice the impulse to walk more quickly or at a more regular pace?

- Did you notice anything different about the left and right sides of your body?

- Have you noticed any benefits from your daily meditation practice over the last six days? In what ways?

Go Deeper

Meditate longer

Monks practicing Walking Meditation will sometimes practice for hours on end! I recommend slowly experimenting with increasing your Walking Meditation by 5-minute increments.

More reflections for your Meditation Notebook

* After practicing Walking Meditation, what do you think Buddhist monk Thich Nhat Hanh meant by saying, "Walk as if you are kissing the Earth with your feet"?

* Are there other areas of your life that might benefit from slow, intentional mindfulness?

* Are there any other familiar hallways or paths in your life where you might consider a Walking Meditation?

Practice sitting and walking

* Another way to practice an extended version of Walking Meditation would be to practice a seated meditation followed by a Walking Meditation.

* If you choose to practice 20 minutes of seated meditation, follow it up with 20 minutes of Walking Meditation.

Mindful driving

- The next time you drive, pay extra-close attention to your field of awareness in all directions.

- Notice all the other drivers and any pedestrians.

- Hold a soft focus, or open awareness, in all directions around you, keeping your concentrated focus on your intention: the direction you are driving in.

- Notice your driving habits. Do you have a tendency to drive mindfully and safely? Do you tend to be in a hurry, pushing or exceeding the posted speed limit?

Recommended Reading

Peace Is Every Step by Thich Nhat Hanh

After the Ecstasy, the Laundry by Jack Kornfield

NOTES: DAY 6

Date: .... Time: ....

Length of meditation: ....

In a few words (e.g., easy, challenging, relaxing, boring), describe how you found this meditation:

....

....

....

....

....

Body Scan Meditation

MEDITATION LENGTH: 15 MINUTES

What Is It?

Body scanning, also known as "sweeping the body," is an important, fundamental mindfulness meditation technique. The purpose of the body scan is to focus in on every area of your body, from head to toe, and explore how each part feels. Here's the catch—you notice how it's feeling, but you don't do anything about it, even if it's uncomfortable. No squirming or itching or judging. ("My foot's asleep—it's screwing up my body scan!") Your only task is to notice.

The practice of a Body Scan Meditation is typically done lying down in a comfortable position. It consists of the meditator mindfully and gradually moving her awareness through each part of the body. While this practice is known to be deeply relaxing (and even a great technique to alleviate insomnia), the deep mind-body connection developed is also a major supporter of the mind-body awareness needed in moving meditations such as yoga and mindful walking.

On Day 1, you focused your awareness on the breath. You counted the breaths, but you also became aware of the many subtle experiences in the body as a result of the breath. This physical awareness will be

exercised and strengthened today by systematically moving it throughout different parts of the body, by "sweeping," or "scanning" the body.

On Day 2, you practiced holding an open awareness of your internal and external environment, and on Day 5 you practiced emotional
awareness. You will be using both those skills today in your Body Scan
Meditation. For example, as your awareness focuses on your left foot,
you will of course notice the physical (or external) sensations being
experienced by your left foot, but you will also notice any thoughts
and emotions (internal sensations) that arise in relation to the physical
sensations. Perhaps you remember hurting your foot at one time, or you
notice thoughts like "I hate the way my feet look."

As with any meditation technique, you will be practicing the skill
of unattached observation and mental noting. Notice the thoughts that
arise, continue breathing, notice any sensory input from the body, and
after a moment, gently guide your awareness to the next body part. In
Body Scan Meditation, the body parts you focus on become the objects
of meditation; they become what you return your awareness to when
your mind inevitably wanders.

Sometimes physical strain is inflicted on certain parts of the body as
a result of poor posture or unhealthy habits. For example, many people
slouch, causing stress on various points along the spine. On the other
hand, another example of poor posture causing strain on the body is
the overcorrection of a slouch (standing up in a "superhero" pose with
the chest out and spine curved backward). Habitual unhealthy eating
causes stress on the heart and digestive system, and smoking causes
stress on the lungs and the entire cardiovascular system. The practice
of body scanning can help bring your awareness to physical stress and
begin the process of self-analysis to alleviate it.

For example, say you are doing a Body Scan Meditation and you
notice a subtle sensation of tightness in your throat. First you bring your
focus deeper into that area and release the tension by taking a slow,
full inhale followed by a slow, full exhale. Then you guide your awareness to the next body part. The analysis begins when you ask yourself

questions like "Why am I feeling tightness in my throat?" You will then notice the thoughts that arise as your subconscious mind attempts to answer your question. It could come clearly and simply, like "The city air I've been breathing is making my throat feel tight." The answer may not come right away, but that's okay; you will have planted the seed of the question in your mind, and your subconscious mind will work to find the answer.

In some cases, it will take regular practice to disengage from chronic tension or stress in certain parts of the body. In those instances, each time you do a body scan, you might ask yourself "Why am I feeling ____ in my ____?" This poses an important question for your subconscious mind, which houses all of your memories and past experiences. With this deeper understanding of yourself and the sensations you carry with you throughout your life, you develop an understanding of what your needs are.

What You'll Get Out of It

Body Scan Meditation is an easy way to practice a technique that has numerous applications. For example, in yoga, the human body is mapped out by a system of **chakras**, in addition to the biological body map. Chakras are energy centers more or less centered along the spinal column. Each energy center is related to a specific physical function, as well as an emotional, spiritual, or practical function. For example, the root chakra is located at the base of the spine where the spine roots down when seated. The root chakra, also called the base chakra or earth chakra, is associated with the adrenal glands. The adrenal glands are commonly known as the producers and releasers of adrenaline—the "fight or flight" hormone. Because of this, the root chakra is related to all things "survival." Identifying adrenal fatigue from a yogic perspective would suggest considering the health of the root chakra and becoming aware of the basic survival needs of home, safety, and security.

In a **chakra balancing** meditation (one of the most popular kinds of Body Scan Meditations), one guides one's awareness through the seven main chakras, taking a moment to consider each energy center, the physical health it is associated with, and the aspects of daily life affected by it. This is done by releasing any tension that arises in your awareness and gently moving on to the next part of the body, breathing life into it and letting go of any stress being placed on that part of the body.

By practicing Body Scan Meditation, you will cultivate:

Deep relaxation and improved sleep **Yoga nidra** (or yogic sleep) is the body scan practice of taking the body into deep relaxation without allowing the mind to drift off to sleep. The standard Body Scan Meditation in today's lesson is almost identical in form to a traditional yoga nidra practice. You will practice keeping your mind alert and present while allowing the body to decompress deeply into an effortless stillness.

Alleviation of insomnia During meditation, you maintain an alert wakefulness. However, an effective application of a body scan is systematically relaxing each part of your body (releasing tension one body part at a time), and simply allowing yourself to fall asleep.

Mind-body connection As you guide your awareness through the body, and each part of the body "joins in" the meditation, it is almost as if each part of the body has its moment in the spotlight. Your conscious awareness will be directed at one body part at a time, and that body part will have its moment to speak to you in subtle ways. The practice of meditation is to really listen, to actively witness what each body part is communicating to you. This practice can become very deep for someone interested in learning about the innate wisdom of the body.

Self-awareness and self-regulation Have you ever met someone who just didn't seem to know her impact on her environment? Maybe she is loud at inopportune moments, or maybe she is insensitive about what she says to others. A Body Scan Meditation can help you become more aware of yourself and your internal processes. For instance, if you notice that you are becoming frustrated, your words are becoming sharper, and the tension in your neck and shoulders is increasing, you have the opportunity to use your awareness to wisely choose words and actions that are in the best interests of your current circumstances. You will have already practiced releasing tension systematically, so you will be able to breathe, find the areas of tension within, let them go, and open your mind to the larger perspective. This can help you make clearer, healthier decisions that your future self will be more than likely glad you did.

Deeper meditation When it comes to deep meditation, the more we can get the body "out of the way," the better. That is to say, discomfort or distractions in the body can keep the mind preoccupied with shallow thoughts of the body's immediate environment. When you practice body scanning, there is direct communication between your mind and each part of your body.

What You'll Need

For today's meditation, as with all meditation techniques, you don't need much to get you going. Today you will need:

- a comfortable place to lie down
  - I recommend lying down on your back, on a rug or mat, with a pillow under your head, a pillow under your knees, and a light blanket on top of you.
  - I don't recommend doing this practice in bed unless you are specifically using it as a tool to help you fall asleep.
- a quiet space to lie where you won't be easily disturbed (by someone walking in on you, for example)

- a timer (if you decide to use the timer on your smartphone, it is best to put the phone on airplane mode or silent to prevent distractions from incoming alerts). Today you will be especially glad of your timer, as the risk of falling asleep is a little higher than usual since you will be lying down.

- your Meditation Notebook and a pen or pencil

Get Started

Meditations, as with most things in life, are first taught using very basic principles. Once the premise is understood, deeper and more complex stages are introduced. Today's meditation will introduce you to this body-awareness practice, which in itself has great benefits. But the deeper practice and its applications are actually quite extensive. Deeper knowledge of human anatomy and the yogic sciences includes massages, postures, and breathing techniques that will bring about different effects on various parts of the body.

We will begin today with our mindfulness-based body scan technique, and in the Go Deeper section, you will be invited to practice an all-body and life-balancing meditation, which will draw a connection between parts of your body and their correlation to daily life.

Please read through this entire meditation before beginning. Ideally you will remember the instructions and not have to interrupt the meditation to check the next step.

BODY SCAN MEDITATION

1. Find a place to lie down where you won't be disturbed.

2. Gather one pillow for under your head, another for under your knees, and a light blanket to cover yourself with.

3. Set your intention: "I am going to commit the next 15 minutes to practicing a Body Scan Meditation. I will mindfully guide my awareness throughout my body; release any tension that may arise; breathe through any sensations, thoughts, or emotions that may come up; accept things as they are; and maintain alert wakefulness of the mind even as my body enters deep relaxation."

BEGIN MEDITATING

1. Set your timer for 15 minutes.

2. Lie down. Take a moment to get yourself comfortable, adjusting the pillows and blanket as necessary. Allow your eyes to gently close.

3. Bring your awareness to the breath, feeling your lungs expand and contract.

4. Allow the only movement in the body to be the breath and the heartbeat.

5. Notice the different sounds and movements in all directions around you.

6. Bring your awareness to your head: your scalp, your forehead, your cheeks, the muscles around your eyes, your lips, and your jaw.

7. With an exhale, release any subtle tension or pressure held anywhere in the head. Give yourself a few breaths here until all the areas of your head feel open, relaxed, and soft.

8. Move your awareness to your neck and shoulders, noticing any sensations or tension.

9. With an exhale, let go of any "holding" or tension in your neck and shoulders.

10. Give yourself a few breaths here until your neck and shoulders feel open, relaxed, and soft.

11. Move your awareness to your upper arms, then lower arms, then hands and fingers, all the way to your fingertips. Take a few breaths, allowing the arms and hands to rest and decompress under their own weight as you exhale.

12. Move your awareness to your chest and upper back. Breathe and release any tension with the exhale.

13. Move your awareness to your belly, hips, and lower back, down through your pelvic bowl and into your thighs.

14. Breathe gently but deeply, in and out through your nose. Notice your thoughts as you gently release any tension in these areas.

15. Move your awareness to your knees, calves, shins, ankles, and feet, all the way to the tips of your toes.

16. Breathe gently but deeply, in and out through your nose. Notice your thoughts as you gently release any tension in these areas.

17. Hold an open awareness of your entire body. Notice when sensations arise, and breathe through them.

18. Rest in stillness. Notice any impulse to fidget or move, but breathe through it, letting go of any tension and overriding the temptation to adjust or move. Practice accepting things as they are.

Wrap Up

When your timer goes off, take note of the sensations and thoughts that came up in your meditation. Take a few deep breaths and slowly begin to move and stretch your body. Oftentimes the final pose in an asana yoga class is a Body Scan Meditation in the posture called **shavasana**, or "corpse pose," which is done lying on your back with palms facing up. Transitioning out of shavasana in a yoga class, you are usually encouraged to roll to one side, take a few breaths on that side, and lift yourself up slowly. Whichever way you decide to get up, what matters is that you give yourself a moment to exit the meditation without a sense of rushing. Transitioning mindfully out of meditation helps you keep the relaxed state developed during your practice, thus extending the "shelf life" of the benefits of calmness, clarity, and openness.

Keep track of your meditation practice in the space provided at the end of the chapter.

If you have time, pick up your Meditation Notebook and make a few notes. When making meditation notes, it's great to always look at them with curiosity, like a scientist. Consider your meditation an experiment. What came up in this meditation? What did you experience? Be present with your journaling, as you would be within the meditation practice itself.

Some questions you might want to ask yourself related to this specific meditation include:

• Were you able to pick up on any sensitivities or sensations in the body that you didn't expect? For example, "I was surprised to notice that several times throughout the meditation, I found myself fidgeting my toes and moving my feet."

• What parts of the body stood out for you in your body scan? For example, "My body was so still that I could feel the pulse of my heart beating in both of my hands."

- Did you notice any thoughts associated with particular parts of the body? For example, "I noticed that when I brought my awareness to my neck and shoulders, I felt tension in my neck, and as I began to release it, I saw images of my neck hunched over looking at my phone or at a computer screen. I thought about how I've been spending more time on my electronic devices than usual."

Go Deeper

Body- and life-balancing meditation on the chakras

The seven primary chakras of the human body are said to address all major functions of the body and the primary factors of human experience. This makes them a powerful tool in creating a life of balance and health. There are many different ways to practice a chakra-balancing meditation, including the mental visualization of different colors in the body, singing of certain notes, or **chanting** of certain words associated with the chakras.

While there are many techniques, the goal is to go through each of the chakras in order, consider the physical body in that area, consider the related aspects of your life, breathe into them, accept things as they are with no judgment, let go of any tension, and then move on to the next chakra.

Here is a quick guide to the seven chakras, the physical body parts they are associated with, and the areas of daily life they are said to relate to.

Crown Chakra (located on the top of the head) is related to the brain stem, the pineal gland in the brain, and is said to govern the individual's sense of spirituality and connection to a higher power.

Third Eye Chakra (located in the center of the forehead) is associated with the "inner eye" of wisdom, knowledge, and understanding.

Throat Chakra (located in the throat) is associated with communication and truth.

Heart Chakra (located in the heart center) is associated with connection to others and the world.

Solar Plexus Chakra (located in the gut) is associated with the center of the severed umbilical cord, where the individual life and free will were first declared as separate from the mother.

Sacral Chakra (located in the sexual organs) is associated with creativity in the biological sense but is also associated with other creative pursuits.

Root Chakra (located at the base of the spine) is related to home, grounding, stability, and survival.

Recommended Reading

Chakra Healing by Margarita Alcantara

Yogalosophy by Mandy Ingber

NOTES: DAY 7

Date: .... Time: ....

Length of meditation: ....

In a few words (e.g., easy, challenging, relaxing, boring), describe
how you found this meditation:

....

....

....

....

....

....

Mantra Meditation

MEDITATION LENGTH: 15 MINUTES

What Is It?

Perhaps one of the most popular meditation techniques found in many cultures all over the world is the repetition of a word or phrase, which we will refer to as a **mantra**.

Mantra, translated from Pali, literally means "mind-vehicle," signaling that the mantra (the word or phrase) is the meditation object on which to rest the mind. Just as in Zazen Breath Awareness Meditation when we focused on the breath, and in the Body Scan Meditation when we focused on physical sensations, the focus of Mantra Meditation is on the word or phrase we choose as a mantra. Mantra-based meditation practices can be found in the Sufi Muslim tradition, Kabbalistic meditation, Christian meditation, Native American chanting, and Hindu and Buddhist meditation.

There are two main methods by which a mantra is used in meditation: silently or out loud. In the mantra-based meditation technique taught by popular modern organizations like Transcendental Meditation, The Veda Center, and The Chopra Center, silent mantras are employed as a meditation object for personal meditation practice. For example, Deepak Chopra, founder of The Chopra Center, often teaches the universal mantra of *so hum*. This mantra was created to be reminiscent of the sound of the inhale (*so*) and exhale (*hum*), and is loosely translated from Pali to mean "I am." In group meditation practice, mantras are often chanted out loud. In Sufi, Kabbalistic, Christian, Native American, Buddhist, and Hindu traditions, there is the practice of audible repetition of sacred prayers, scriptures, and other mantras.

In addition to these two main methods, there are two main *kinds* of mantras that can be used: meaningful or meaningless. In most traditions, the meaning of the mantra is very important. This is especially true in the traditions that chant sacred prayers or names of deities. However, in Vedic Meditation and Transcendental Meditation, the emphasis is placed on the mantra technique rather than the meaning of the mantra. For this reason, the chosen mantras in these traditions are typically in a language not spoken by the meditator, which allows the meditator to focus on the sound of the mantra rather than its perceived meaning.

An example of a meaningful mantra is the use of an **affirmation**. An affirmation is a statement of truth ("affirming that which is true"), repeated either out loud or silently in the mind.

A few examples of affirmations are:

"I am ready for anything."

"I am happy."

"I am successful."

"I am open to seeing things differently."

"I am healthy."

The thoughts that arise when using a meaningful versus a meaningless mantra will differ widely. Typically, thoughts that arise when using a supposedly meaningless mantra, such as one in another language, will be thoughts already occupying your subconscious mind, ready and waiting to make themselves known to you. In contrast, when using a meaningful mantra, the thoughts that arise will typically be related to the mantra itself. For example, your mantra may be "I am happy and healthy." The thoughts that come to your mind will both support and reject this statement. You will become aware of the subtle notions you have underneath the surface of awareness; the thoughts that "agree" with this affirmation will be affirmed, and the thoughts that "disagree" with this affirmation will also make themselves known. The practice is to observe all the thoughts while continuing to declare the affirmation. Whenever the mind strays from the mantra (whether it is being spoken out loud or silently repeated), the awareness should always return to the mantra.

What You'll Get Out of It

Mantra Meditation is one of the most basic and widely used forms of meditation, and with good reason. It is easy to practice and has some very powerful effects. By practicing Mantra Meditation, you will be able to:

Rewire your brain Every thought we have and every conclusion we come to is the result of neurons firing through specific routes in the brain, called **neural pathways**. When we hold positive affirmations in the mind, especially if we can really believe them (as opposed to the rote repetition of words), the brain creates new neural pathways. There is little research demonstrating exactly how many times we have to think or experience something before it becomes our default mode, but we do have evidence that the repetition of words and behaviors eventually creates new neural pathways. As our affirmations impact our emotional body, and our actions begin to reflect the affirmations, new habits are developed and a new way of being can be experienced.

Focus and concentrate better The practice of holding focused attention on one object and consistently redirecting the awareness back to that one object whenever the mind wanders is strengthening the "attention muscle." When using a mantra, you still hold your awareness on all the sensory input of the moment, but your focus is directed and settled on the mantra. This gives you the subtle ability to stay focused even in other areas of life. Think of your mantra as a symbol for your "purpose." An analogy example I often appreciate is this: When you're driving in traffic, your purpose is to go along the route to your destination safely. As you drive, someone cuts you off. Someone cutting you off is like your mind wandering off the mantra. If you're not careful, it could derail your mood for the entire day. Simply notice that the other driver cut you off and get back to your route. Practicing Mantra Meditation can help you get back to your purpose more quickly.

Reduce stress and anxiety The practice of a mantra immediately takes your mental attention away from the outside world and concentrates it on the mantra. Taking a brief mental break away from the source of stress and anxiety is a great strategy for reducing the impact of these influences on your life. Directing the conscious awareness to the mantra (whether meaningless or meaningful), gives it something new to focus on. If the mantra is a positive affirmation, it gives the mind something positive to attend to. If the mantra is meaningless, it still gives the mind a reference point on neutral ground to "take a break" from stressors.

Drop in to meditation faster Many meditation schools recommend using the same mantra over an extended period of time to simplify the process and avoid "contemplation on the meaning" of meditation. By establishing a consistent relationship with a specific mantra, consistent practitioners of these traditions report being able to "drop in" to deep meditation faster through the use of their trusty mantra. One of my students who has routinely used the same mantra for years once told me, "My mantra feels like a magic word; as soon as I start to repeat it in my mind, I click right into a meditative state." While you may not have this experience right away, consistent use of the same mantra is widely known to have this effect.

What You'll Need

For today's meditation, as with all meditation techniques, you don't need much to get you going. Whether you sit on the floor or a chair is up to you and often depends on where you decide to practice—home, work, etc. Each day may be different as well, depending on how you're feeling. Today you will need:

* a comfortable chair or cushion where you can sit with your spine comfortably erect

* a quiet place to sit where you won't be easily disturbed (by someone walking in on you, for example)

* a timer (if you decide to use the timer on your smartphone, it is best to put the phone on airplane mode or silent to prevent distractions from incoming alerts)

* your Meditation Notebook and a pen or pencil

Get Started

As I mentioned, there are numerous ways to approach this technique. While these practices essentially develop the same skillset, there are subtleties that set them apart. For example, in an audible repetition of a Sanskrit mantra, meditative focus is placed on the experience of the vibration of the mantra as the meditator "chants" the mantra out loud.

By contrast, in an audible repetition of an affirmation, emphasis is generally placed on the creative visualization of the affirmation in full form. For example, if my mantra is "I am happy and healthy," my meditative focus should be on "seeing" and "feeling" happy and healthy.

For our practice today, we will be saying aloud a very simple mantra: "om" or "aum," which in many traditions is known as the primordial sound, or the cumulative sound of the entire universe at once. We will break this mantra down into its three audible parts (*ah, uu, mm*) and will begin by using one syllable at a time before bringing them all together. In the Go Deeper section, I offer up ways to use affirmations and silent mantras.

Please read through this entire meditation before beginning. Ideally you will remember the instructions and not have to interrupt the meditation to check the next step.

MANTRA MEDITATION

BEFORE MEDITATING

1. Find a place to sit where you won't be disturbed.

2. Take a moment to get into a comfortable seated position, spine erect, that you will be able to maintain for the duration of the practice with as little movement or adjustment as possible.

3. Set your intention: "I am going to commit the next 15 minutes to practice Mantra Meditation. I will focus on the experience of the vibration inside my body, as well as the thoughts, emotions, and sensations that arise."

BEGIN MEDITATING

1. Set your timer for 15 minutes.

2. Allow your eyes to gently close.

3. Bring your awareness to the breath.

4. As your body settles into a relaxed state, begin to release a gentle *mm* on the exhale. Allow the entire exhale from start to finish to have an audible *mm* . . .

5. Notice the vibration of the humming through your throat, mouth, neck, and chest.

6. Continue for a few more breaths, chanting the humming sound, just on the exhale.

7. Feel the vibration throughout your body and in your mind's eye, perhaps even visualizing the sound vibrations echoing in all directions out beyond the body.

8. Now, for the next few breaths, on the exhale, release the *ah* sound. *Ahhh* . . . Allow your throat to be relaxed and open.

9. Notice the sound vibrations as they move throughout the body. Do this for a few breaths.

10. Feel the vibrations, and visualize them moving beyond the body in all directions around you.

11. After a few breaths exhaling *ah*, move to the *uu* sound (as in *true*).

12. Gently exhale *uu*, allowing it to extend through the entire exhale.

13. Experience the vibrations, notice the thoughts coming to mind, and continue to exhale *uu* for a few more breaths.

14. For the rest of the meditation, until your timer goes off, put all three syllables together: "ah" "uu" "mm." On the exhale, release the sound "aum," giving each letter somewhat equal audible time. This doesn't need to be perfect, but try to find some balance.

15. Follow the vibrations throughout your body, holding an open awareness of any sensations, emotions, or thoughts that might arise.

16. Continue with *aum* until your timer goes off.

Wrap Up

When you finish, take a few deep breaths in silence before getting up. Exit your meditation without rushing. Transitioning mindfully out of meditation helps you keep the relaxed state developed during your practice, thus extending the "shelf life" of the benefits of calmness, clarity, and openness.

Because of the multiple ways of approaching the use of a mantra in meditation, I recommend revisiting this technique as open-mindedly as possible and adjusting your approach by trying it different ways, with different kinds of mantras.

Keep track of your meditation practice in the space provided at the end of the chapter.

If you have time, take a few minutes to write down your answers to the following prompts in your Meditation Notebook:

- Before today, had you heard of Mantra Meditation? Was your experience what you expected?

- Take a moment to review the different syllables you used in this meditation. Did you notice anything different about each of them? For example, did *ah* seem to feel differently in the body than *mm*? The more detailed you are in your journaling now, the more clearly you will be able to look back at your progress and any changes that may have happened in your practice.

- The scientific study of sound wave phenomena is called **cymatics**. In cymatics, a form of sound therapy is used to direct sound waves into different parts of the body using tuning forks, music speakers, and even the human voice. Some cymatic self-treatments are done just like today's Mantra Meditation, by humming, chanting, or "toning" certain sounds or syllables to send a consistent sound vibration throughout the body. In your journal, describe the sensation of the sound vibrations as you chanted your mantra. In what parts of the body were they most prominent? Did it feel relaxing, energizing, or something else?

- Journal anything else that may come to mind, keeping track of your experience. You will refer to these notes when building your meditation practice.

Go Deeper

Silent Mantra Meditation

- Take 15 minutes and practice a meditation using a silent mantra.

- Use the same general guidelines as today's meditation, except do not make any noise. All mantras will be silently repeated within.

- For this meditation, use the Pali words *so hum*.

- As you practice the meditation, you will pair *so* with your inhale and *hum* with your exhale.

- When you notice that your mind has wandered from the mantra, which you will know by the fact that you are thinking anything other than the mantra, simply return to the mantra, silently repeating *so* with every inhale and *hum* with every exhale.

- When your timer goes off, journal your experience with the silent mantra.

Affirmation tips

An affirmation can be used like a silent mantra in meditation, or it can be used as a constant reminder. For example, a business owner's mantra may be "I provide an excellent service for an excellent price."

Take a moment to consider an affirmation that supports your current goals. This should be written in the present tense and from a positive perspective. For example, rather than saying "I will be more responsible with my finances," say "I am responsible with my finances," or rather than saying "I don't eat unhealthy foods," say "I eat healthy foods."

Write your affirmation down somewhere you will see it daily—maybe on a notepad at your desk or on your nightstand, your bathroom mirror, or a card in your wallet. Throughout your day, silently repeat to yourself your positive affirmation, visualizing a successful result and allowing it to keep you mentally and emotionally focused on your goals, regardless of any challenges that may come up.

Recommended Reading

Transcendental Meditation by Jack Forem

The Book of Secrets by Deepak Chopra

Living with Intent by Mallika Chopra

Unplug by Suze Yalof Schwartz

NOTES: DAY 8

Date: .... Time: ....

Length of meditation: ....

Posture: ....

Mudra used (if applicable): ....

In a few words (e.g., easy, challenging, relaxing, boring), describe how you found this meditation:

....

....

....

....

....

....

"We don't sit in meditation to become good meditators. We sit in meditation so that we'll be more awake in our lives."

Pema Chodron

Sitting with Difficult Emotions

MEDITATION LENGTH: 20 MINUTES

What Is It?

We all carry around with us some level of difficult emotion we have to deal with in our daily lives. These unpleasant emotions can come from failed relationships, workplace stressors, or any number of other life circumstances. Sitting with difficult emotions is a practice of mindfully acknowledging challenging feelings and accepting the experience of them rather than avoiding, resisting, or numbing ourselves to them. On Day 5: Observing Your Emotions, you noticed the ebb and flow of your emotional state—simply watching your emotions as they came and went. Today you take this skill to the next level, deepening your emotional strength by addressing your fear of and resistance to difficult emotions.

We have all survived challenging experiences. What happens when we make it to the other side of those challenges? We emerge forever changed by them. We learn from them, and if we stay open to what our challenges have to teach us, we grow. Today's meditation is on the emotions surrounding these kinds of challenging experiences. These are the emotions that we tend to prefer to avoid, such as guilt, frustration, sadness, anger, loneliness, spite, and shame. Learning to turn *toward* these emotions, instead of away, is an incredibly powerful practice because it really gives you the upper hand!

Much of the time, we live at the whim of life and its circumstances— and difficult feelings come up when something triggers us. In the practice of sitting with difficult emotions, you will choose to face the challenging emotions on *your* terms, at the time and place of *your* choosing. There is a lot of power in that. Think of it as having the "home court advantage" in the duel between you and life's challenges. Bear in mind that the emotions themselves aren't causing the challenges that you associate with them. The emotions are triggered by circumstances and caused by our fears, insecurities, ignorance, past experiences, and anxieties. Difficult emotions arise, often unexpectedly, and cloud our ability to deal effectively with our current circumstances. In such circumstances, our first priority should be to establish emotional self-regulation so that we can think as clearly as possible.

Today is Day 9 of your meditation program, and you may have noticed by now that I always suggest that you find a quiet place to practice where you are unlikely to be disturbed or interrupted. This is, in part, to set you up for success in the event that difficult emotions come up during meditation. If you are in a safe place, alone at home, in a meditative state, and difficult emotions arise, you will likely see the circumstances of your challenges from a more coherent perspective than if those same difficult emotions were to arise at work, in public, or with another person.

What You'll Get Out of It

Sitting with difficult emotions can be one of the simplest yet most powerful things you can do to enhance and improve your life experience. By practicing this meditation, you will cultivate:

Emotional maturity Think of the sensationalized news and the false scarcity promoted by popular marketing tactics—modern life has a tendency to strike a sense of urgency, deprivation, and hurriedness in just about everybody. We're all so busy going from one place to the next that we rarely give ourselves the opportunity to process the deep, profound changes occurring in our personal lives as well as on the national and global stage. When we do find ourselves discussing these things, we rarely leave the discussion feeling satisfied and whole. These are signs of emotional immaturity. The way we are socialized has conditioned us to be mostly numb to the depths of human emotion we are all subject to and capable of. **Emotional maturity** comes only through experience and openness to what experience teaches, and when it does come, everything changes. Emotionally mature people are clear thinking, compassionate, and wise, drawing from the depths of their experiences to face challenges, solve problems, and fix mistakes.

Less reactive responses Being triggered into an emotional response can cause irreparable damage to relationships or careers and can waste precious resources, such as time. However, dedicating time to allowing challenging emotions to arise is actually very efficient. Of course, I am in no way advocating ignoring or suppressing an emotion when it comes up naturally. But making a practice of allowing difficult emotions to be felt in meditation helps overcome the knee-jerk reactivity of modern life and can open our minds to insight into the true nature of our experiences. You will become less reactive and less "startled" by difficult emotions when they arise. Think of it this way: If you are regularly expressing yourself and experiencing a wide range of emotions in a safe place, you will have no build-up of tension or pressure to explode when you get triggered. You will reduce your chances of saying or doing things in the emotional intensity of the moment that you will later regret.

Recovery of your emotional power With the power of the Internet in the palm of our hand, we have access to content that can trigger just about any emotion. This means we can have the entire spectrum of our emotions triggered by the simple tap of a screen. From the most beautiful HD photos of islands to chaotic footage of war tragedy, we have very little real control over what we are exposed to in today's world. One way of looking at this meditation practice is that you are giving yourself the opportunity to sit in private with your emotions, understand them, and understand what you need to say or do next, without letting the intensity of the emotions direct you to take reactive or unskilled actions.

Self-knowledge and understanding Sitting with difficult emotions can help us identify their source. Being able to sit with your difficult emotions gives you the ability to begin to interact with them and question them. For example, "Am I feeling depressed and sad today because of personal circumstances, or because of the many tragic and dramatic news stories I've been watching?"

What You'll Need

For today's meditation, as with all meditation techniques, you don't need much to get you going. Whether you sit on the floor or a chair is up to you and often depends on where you decide to practice—home, work, etc. Each day may be different as well, depending on how you're feeling. Today you will need:

- a comfortable chair or cushion where you can sit with your spine comfortably erect

- a quiet place to sit where you won't be easily disturbed (by someone walking in on you, for example)

- a timer (if you decide to use the timer on your smartphone, it is best to put the phone on airplane mode or silent to prevent distractions from incoming alerts)

- your Meditation Notebook and a pen or pencil

IF YOU START TO FEEL OVERWHELMED

This meditation may eventually—or for some people immediately—call up painful feelings or trigger painful memories that cause you to feel overwhelmed. If that happens to you, there are a couple of ways to dial back those immediate feelings of sadness, fear, or whatever your emotion is. The simplest way is to gently end the session by opening your eyes and taking a few deep breaths. Sit quietly, breathing, until you begin to feel more peaceful. Another way to regain your footing is to gently move your awareness from the difficult emotion to another aspect of your in-the-moment experience, like your breath, physical sensations, or sounds you hear around you. You can use meditation techniques you've already learned to help you through a challenging sit.

Get Started

In this meditation you will recall a time when you experienced a negative emotion. If you have suffered a major loss or trauma in your past, don't start with that—pick something less upsetting, such as an intimidating presentation at work or an argument you've had recently. Exploring trauma is best done with the help of a professional, and you don't want to become overwhelmed—that isn't the point of this practice.

Please read through this entire meditation before beginning. Ideally you will remember the instructions and not have to interrupt the meditation to check the next step.

SITTING WITH DIFFICULT EMOTIONS

BEFORE MEDITATING

1. Find a place to sit where you won't be disturbed.

2. Take a moment to get yourself into a comfortable sitting position, spine erect, that you will be able to maintain for the duration of the practice with as little movement or adjustment as possible.

3. Set your intention: "I am going to commit the next 20 minutes to practice sitting with difficult emotions in meditation. I know that I am in a safe place, and I choose to allow any difficult emotions to come up, knowing that if at any point it becomes too much for me, I can simply open my eyes."

BEGIN MEDITATING

1. Set your timer for 20 minutes.

2. Allow your eyes to gently close.

3. Bring your awareness to the breath.

4. Allow the exhale to send a wave of decompression throughout the body, letting go of any tension, almost like a one-second body scan.

5. Give yourself a moment to really let go of any resistance and become open and relaxed.

6. Begin to notice how you feel right now. This may take a moment. Are you feeling happy? Bored? Angry? Indifferent?

7. Simply notice and acknowledge however you're feeling now. (For example, "I feel hopeful.")

8. Now recall a recent time when you felt a negative emotion like anger or sadness.

9. Where were you when you felt the emotion? Recall your physical surroundings.

10. What did you do when you felt that feeling? Did you yell? Cry? Do nothing?

11. Now notice how you feel in this moment—you are likely feeling that same way again. Allow yourself to experience it as an experiment to understand it better, knowing that it is temporary.

12. Resist the urge to story-tell. (For example, "If Mark hadn't been late, I wouldn't have gotten so mad.")

13. Explore the quality of the emotion you feel. Is there more than one thing present? Is it anger *and* fear? Anxiety *and* loneliness?

14. Acknowledge and name the emotions you feel as they arise in your awareness. (For example, "I feel angry" or just "Anger.")

15. Repeat the acknowledgment until you notice the feeling begin to subside. If it does, notice the next feeling that rises in your awareness.

16. Maintain mindful awareness of your emotional state, any sensations in the body, and any thoughts arising in the mind.

17. Continue breathing through anything that comes up, seeing yourself as capable of containing complex, difficult emotions within your field, seeing yourself as a poised, unshakable, compassionate, strong, confident person.

By establishing the mental notion that you are emotionally capable, you grant yourself the capacity to move through any emotional state that comes up. This meditation is a great one to attempt when in the midst of emotional drama.

Wrap Up

I studied with grief expert David Kessler, and in his Healing Grief seminar, we were paired off for an exercise in which we sat across from our partner and shared with them our experiences of heartbreak and loss. None of the traditional go-to comforting tactics were allowed: We were instructed not to respond verbally, not to offer a tissue, not to touch or hug. We were instructed to simply bear witness to the grief of our partners, and they to ours. This was because actions like offering a tissue or a hug interrupts the individual's expression of grief, rather than allowing that person to express and release it fully. I found the experience to be deeply healing, and I find it to be healing whether I'm sitting across from someone or not. I have found that sitting with grief or other difficult emotions in meditation and bearing witness to one's own negative emotions can be an extraordinary act of self-care, providing a deep sense of release and healing.

Sometimes during a meditation like this one, some of our most primal emotions can come up. An old grudge can rear its ugly head, past circumstances we haven't "gotten over yet" come to mind, we recall roadblocks and heartbreak. In many cases, the very thing we've been trying to ignore or hide from will be the very thing that comes up during the meditation. It is a part of this meditation practice for things to unfold this way. This is a training exercise in establishing mental and emotional resilience so that we can embody and contain deeper levels of understanding and strength.

In her book *Tears to Triumph*, Marianne Williamson derives examples from Judaism, Christianity, and Buddhism alike to demonstrate how suffering has been known since ancient times to provide deep wisdom. This is also true of many indigenous cultures all over the world; in fact, it is a belief common across indigenous cultures of North and South America, Africa, and Southeast Asia that people struck by lightning or affected by other very serious catastrophes of health or safety would, through the experience, have developed deep wisdom and been given "great medicine" by the experience itself, if they were able to emerge from the experience psychologically intact.

Keep track of your meditation practice in the space provided at the end of the chapter.

Using the questions below as prompts, make a few notes in your Meditation Notebook about what came up for you on your journey today. Be as truthful as possible. These notes are your meditation records to help you self-assess your process. The more thorough you are in your journaling, the more you will learn from it.

- Did any individuals come to mind?

- Do you still feel bitter, angry, or upset when you think of them?

- Were you surprised at the negative emotions that came up?

- Did you feel yourself allow them to come up?

- Was there some underlying resistance from within, allowing the emotion to only partially manifest itself?

Go Deeper

Writing Meditation for letting go of an old grievance or grudge

- During your meditation, did someone come to mind who harmed or offended you or someone you care about? Take a sheet of paper and write them a letter. Don't worry, no one will ever see this but you, but it may help if you visualize them receiving it while you write it.

- Explain to them clearly and directly what exactly you are upset about.

- Be honest, mature, wise, and brave. Write out exactly how you feel, even if it takes a few sentences. Be as detailed as you like; the more detailed, the better.

- After you have said what you needed to say, write the following with deep sincerity: "I know that the past cannot be changed. I choose to let go of my grudge and let go of my grievance. I let go of my judgments against you, against myself, and against everyone involved. I am not condoning wrong actions, but I am letting go of the weight of the difficult emotions surrounding this circumstance, accepting that things are as they are, and moving forward in my life."

- Sign the letter.

- Take a moment in meditation and visualize them receiving it. Take a few deep breaths before tearing it up, throwing it away, or burning it as an act of letting go and moving on.

Recommended Reading

Tears to Triumph by Marianne Williamson

You Can Heal Your Heart by David Kessler and Louise Hay

When Things Fall Apart by Pema Chödrön

NOTES: DAY 9

Date: .... Time: ....

Length of meditation: ....

Posture: ....

Mudra used (if applicable): ....

In a few words (e.g., easy, challenging, relaxing, boring), describe how you found this meditation:

....

....

....

....

....

"Afflictive emotions—our jealousy, anger, hatred, fear—can be put to an end. When you realize that these emotions are only temporary, that they always pass on like clouds in the sky, you also realize they can ultimately be abandoned."

the Dalai Lama

Lovingkindness Meditation

MEDITATION LENGTH: 20 MINUTES

What Is It?

The Buddha's practice of **Lovingkindness** or **Heartfulness** Meditation is a mindfulness-based practice that will expand your capacity to see (and even feel) things from a different perspective, through a very intentional technique of invoking a direct experience of unconditional love. In Lovingkindness Meditation, you'll work to cultivate an unconditional, all-inclusive love for all things—people, pets, bugs, trees, the earth, and yourself. It's a tall order, but don't worry, you'll start small. This technique is particularly popular with those who appreciate the work of Jesus Christ and the "new commandment" he gives in John 13:34 that instructs his followers to "love one another." The benefits of lovingkindness practice are amazing: Among other things, a number of studies of practitioners of Lovingkindness Meditation have found measurable brain structure change (increased gray matter volume) in the area of the brain known for cognitive functioning, empathy, social interaction, and emotional processing.

At first glance, this meditation seems simple, but it can reveal unexpected challenges. I once had a student who admitted, "You know, the

Lovingkindness Meditation gets a lot easier when I don't have to send the lovingkindness to myself." I responded, "That's why we begin and end there." As surprising as her statement might be—that she struggles with the *receiving* aspect of lovingkindness—what's even more shocking is that this is not an uncommon sentiment. We often harbor negative self-talk, harsh self-criticism, and in some cases, even traces of self-hatred. There is a healthy place for self-awareness, which helps us grow, make amends, and heal from past mistakes, but if you're having trouble feeling open to receiving lovingkindness, even in the safety and privacy of your own meditation, you are likely being too hard on yourself in your life generally.

The Lovingkindness Meditation begins with cultivating a sense of self-acceptance and unconditional love for your **true self**, regardless of perceived imperfections, regardless of foibles or personality defects, regardless of past mistakes, and regardless of anything (really, any-thing). Unconditional, unending love, all for you. Create your own little **love zone**. Once you're really feeling it, you then invite to mind those who have cared deeply for you: your loved ones, close family members, friends, and even pets, inviting them into the unconditional love zone with you. This is when the fun begins! Next, keeping an open heart and open mind, invite your more casual acquaintances into your thoughts—your neighbors, coworkers, and colleagues—and love them up in your heart and mind. Then you invite to mind strangers, public figures, and, perhaps most importantly, those with whom you have difficulty. Finally, you expand your love zone to include all people, all animals, all plants, all planets, all stars, and all living beings throughout the cosmos.

This practice is about going deep within and accessing the authentic experience of unconditional acceptance and compassion for yourself, then gradually expanding the field of unconditional love outward to include your family, social and professional circles, and beyond into the entire universe.

What You'll Get Out of It

In many ways, Lovingkindness Meditation is the culmination of many of the first nine meditation techniques in this program. It requires focused concentration (Day 1), open awareness (Day 2), observing your emotions (Day 5), and sitting with difficult emotions (Day 9). Today you will also generate positive emotions, stretch your perspective, and experiment with your ability to see things differently, to open your mind to deeper and fuller truths and come to terms with a deep, genuine sense of self-acceptance.

By practicing Lovingkindness Meditation, you will cultivate:

Increased positive emotions and good physical health Positive psychology researcher Dr. Barbara Fredrickson published her findings that regular Lovingkindness Meditation was linked to an increase in overall good physical health and an increase in "a wide range of positive emotions, including love, joy, gratitude, contentment, hope, pride, interest, amusement and awe."

Reduced pain Studies have shown that Lovingkindness Meditation ameliorates migraines, chronic pain, and decreases anger, emotional tension, and psychological distress associated with pain.

Reduced stress Lovingkindness Meditation seems to take the meditator on a mental tour through the bigger picture, finding a natural sense of proportion in the grand scheme of things for our many personal challenges. Paired with the physical relaxation that comes with a mindfulness practice, a sense of calmness and wisdom replaces the grip of tension and stress. Some studies even showed Lovingkindness Meditation to be effective in treating depression and PTSD in veterans.

Reduced inflammation One study also showed a stark decrease in inflammation in those who practice Lovingkindness Meditation on a daily basis.

Better communication with others and empathy Gray matter volume in the brain was shown to be greatly increased in experienced practitioners of Lovingkindness Meditation, specifically in the para-hippocampal gyrus, which is thought to be associated with empathy, understanding of social context, and verbal communication.

Self-compassion and acceptance In the practice of Heartfulness Meditation, we begin and end by giving and receiving lovingkindness to and for ourselves. This is a crucial aspect of the practice in order for the sincere bonding experience this meditation technique generates to take place. The quality of the self-compassion, self-acceptance, and unconditional love that can be felt and received directly influences the following stages of the meditation. A deep sense of self-forgiveness and self-acceptance is a powerful healing experience and can open doors within one's own mind that may have been closed due to self-judgment and self-sabotage.

Longevity Many studies on mood and positive emotion support the notion that positive emotions, like the ones generated by Loving-kindness Meditation, add to not only the quality of your life but also possibly even the length of your life. This is supported by a Harvard Medical School study showing that practitioners of Lovingkindness Meditation had longer telomere length than their non-meditating peers, which is said to be a biological marker for aging.

What You'll Need

Today you will need:

- a comfortable chair or cushion where you can sit with your spine comfortably erect

- a quiet place to sit where you won't be easily disturbed (by someone walking in on you, for example)

- a timer (if you decide to use the timer on your smartphone, it is best to put the phone on airplane mode or silent to prevent distractions from incoming alerts)

- your Meditation Notebook and a pen or pencil

Get Started

Traditionally, there are certain sentences or phrases that are memorized and repeated throughout the practice as an extension of lovingkindness first to yourself, then to all others, and finally to all the world. We will call these sentences the "Heartfulness Mantra." There are many variations on the specific wording, but the core message is the same. Here is my favorite version:

May your mind know truth and your heart know love.
May you be free from harm and free from causing harm.
May you and all your relations be strong, healthy,
happy, and fulfilled,
for the benefit of all beings.

If you like, you are welcome to hold this book open in your lap to glance down at the Heartfulness Mantra for reference. These words can be said out loud, silently in the mind, or you can simply visualize the concept of lovingkindness as an illuminating quality filling the hearts and minds of everyone who enters your thoughts during your meditation.

LOVINGKINDNESS MEDITATION

BEFORE MEDITATING

1. Find a place to sit where you won't be disturbed.

2. Take a moment to get into a comfortable position that you will be able to maintain for the duration of the practice with as little movement or adjustment as possible.

3. Decide whether you will:

    *   Speak the lovingkindness statements out loud.

    *   Repeat the lovingkindness statements silently in your mind.

    *   Simply visualize lovingkindness, happiness, joy, health, clarity, and goodness.

4. Set your intention: "I am going to commit the next 20 minutes to practice Lovingkindness Meditation. I will freely give and receive this gift of unconditional lovingkindness to everyone who comes to mind, without exception. I will remain present for all of my subtle reactions and experiences throughout this process."

BEGIN MEDITATING

1. Set your timer for 20 minutes.

2. Allow your eyes to gently close.

3. Bring your awareness to the experience of the breath. Take a few gentle, deep breaths, settling in and becoming very present.

4. As you inhale, feel the sensation of lovingkindness fill your body.

5. Briefly allow your awareness to sweep over the body, bringing lovingkindness to every one of your limbs, bones, muscles, organs, and cells.

6. Receive and visualize lovingkindness shining from deep within you, in all directions around you, and repeat the Heartfulness Mantra directed toward yourself. ("May my mind know truth and my heart know love.")

7. It can be helpful to bring to mind happy childhood memories of play and laughter.

8. Now, invite to mind someone you find very easy to love: a pet, a baby, a close loved one. Send them unlimited lovingkindness, repeating the Heartfulness Mantra.

9. Invite to mind all the many people you love dearly, sending them lovingkindness, visualizing them shining bright with it, and/or repeating the Heartfulness Mantra.

10. Repeat as different faces come to mind.

11. Don't rush; allow this to feel natural and gradual, not forced.

12. Feel free to spend an additional moment with certain individuals if you wish.

13. Think of your friends, colleagues, coworkers. Repeat the mantra. Send them lovingkindness.

14. Notice any changes in your body, and breathe through them. Try to allow the only movement in the body to be the breath and the heartbeat.

15. Maintain a relaxed stillness—this can be challenging when more difficult "faces" come to mind.

16. Think of someone in pain. Send them lovingkindness. Repeat the mantra.

17. Bring to mind strangers, public figures, and those with whom you have difficulty. Breathe through any resistance, visualize them healthy and happy, send them lovingkindness, and repeat the mantra.

18. Think of all the people all over the world.

19. Think of all the animals all over the world.

20. Think of all the plants, oceans, rivers, streams, mountains, valleys, plains, and cities all over the world. Repeat the mantra for them all.

21. Think of all the planets and stars and all the unknown places and beings far out in the universe, in all directions. Repeat the mantra for them all.

22. Breathe deeply into yourself, cultivating a feeling of being connected to others and the universe. Repeat the mantra for yourself once more.

23. Rest in mindful stillness until your timer goes off.

Wrap Up

As always, end your meditation gently and mindfully. Give yourself a moment to exit the meditation without a sense of rushing. This will help you carry your calm, focused state of mind forward into your day.

Keep track of your meditation practice in the space provided at the end of the chapter.

The real first step in a Lovingkindness Meditation is to take a moment to consider what unconditional love is. Abstract concepts like compassion and love can be spoken of and described, but the key to this kind of practice is in the actual embodiment of the concepts. This means to really feel it inside you. Give yourself some unhurried time with your Meditation Notebook, using the following prompts:

- Who are some individuals to whom you find it very easy to offer lovingkindness? (For example, "Most of my memories with my grandmother are very positive, so when she comes to mind, it inspires feelings of joy, love, and kindness. It is easy for me to offer lovingkindness to her.")

- What are some other images you could call to mind to make it easy for you to experience the feeling of lovingkindness? (Think, "These are a few of my favorite things . . .")

- The real power of a Lovingkindness Meditation is activated when you are able to invoke from within yourself the feeling of loving-kindness and direct it to someone with whom you may have had difficulty—whether it be someone you know or even a public figure you don't like.

- Whose faces were some of the most challenging that came to mind during this practice? (For example, "A politician I really can't stand came to mind, and that was tough! However, I was able to breathe through the initial shock and see through the personality defects and extend my unconditional love long enough for someone else to come to mind next!")

- Give yourself some time to write out anything else that came up for you. Was it easy for you to offer lovingkindness? Was it easy for you to receive it for yourself?

Go Deeper

Lovingkindness Writing Meditation

Open your journal to a fresh page. Write the Heartfulness Mantra at the top or in the center of the page. Take your time writing the mantra, allow it to be intentional and clear, even beautifully written. Set a timer for 10 to 20 minutes. Close your eyes and cultivate lovingkindness within. Once you are feeling the love, open your eyes and begin writing down every name that comes to mind. The names can be written on the lines, off the lines, written quickly or slowly, any way you'd like. Sign and date the page.

Lovingkindness Walking Meditation

On Day 6 we practiced a Walking Meditation. This one is a little bit different. Practice mindful walking, and in addition to directing your focus into the sights, sounds, and sensations of the experience, silently extend the Heartfulness Mantra out to everyone and everything you see.

Lovingkindness Body Scan Meditation

On Day 7 we learned a Body Scan Meditation that involves lying down and sweeping your awareness through the body. In this variation, instead of simply releasing tension throughout every part of the body, you take a moment to offer lovingkindness to each part of the body, visualizing it illuminated with health and vitality.

Lovingkindness Meditation for work, school, or group

Take the time to consider your coworkers, the students and faculty of your school, or the participants in your teams and community activities. Choose one group at a time and offer every single person involved who comes to mind unconditional lovingkindness. You don't need to tell them you did it—but they might be grateful if you did!

Lovingkindness Meditation for family healing

Hold in front of you a family photo. Take a moment to offer each family member lovingkindness individually. If your family is like so many others, there are many things that need to be forgiven, let go of, and accepted. Many families also have a hard time effectively communicating their genuine love and appreciation for one another. Notice the thoughts passing through your mind as you send each individual family member unconditional lovingkindness. And as always, journal after your practice.

Recommended Reading

Real Love by Sharon Salzberg

On Love and Loneliness by Jiddu Krishnamurti

True Love by Thich Nhat Hanh

You Are the Universe by Deepak Chopra and Menas Kafatos

NOTES: DAY 10

Date: .... Time: ....

Length of meditation: ....

Posture: ....

Mudra used (if applicable): ....

In a few words (e.g., easy, challenging, relaxing, boring), describe
how you found this meditation:

....

....

....

....

....

....

Building Your
New Practice

Putting It All Together

Congratulations! You are now a practicing meditator. Sticking with something new like this can be challenging, but you did it. You have taken the first step and begun the process. Take a moment to appreciate this gift you've given yourself—and those around you. After all, the best gift we can give those we love is showing up in our relationships as a better version of ourselves.

By now you have gone on a journey through 10 different meditation techniques. Which techniques are the right ones to take with you moving forward? With as much new information as you've learned, and with such subtle differences between the techniques, it can be a little difficult to decide what your ongoing practice will be now that you've completed the 10-day program and will be meditating on your own. If the use of a daily guide like this one has been helpful for you, you may want to begin again at Day 1 as you continue to develop your habit of daily meditation. Recall that each day has at least one Go Deeper practice that can make your meditation a little more challenging. Did you experiment with any of those throughout the last 10 days? If not, that could be a great place to start.

For those ready to begin a consistent habit, here's how to create a sustainable meditation practice so you can keep reaping the benefits for years to come.

Customizing Your Practice

For a daily practice, I recommend establishing a consistent time and place for meditating undisturbed. This is your personal time, and the time designated for your meditation practice should be prioritized by you and honored by those around you.

In my experience, the easier I make my morning meditation on myself, the more likely I am to actually practice. The way I do this is by having my meditation cushion set up, ready to go at all times. As soon as I wake up in the morning, I walk directly to my meditation cushion and immediately meditate. Throughout the day, if I'm feeling stressed, overstimulated, or emotional, I simply take a few minutes on the cushion to regulate myself.

Everyone is different, so of course our meditation practices will be different, too. Review what you've written in your Meditation Notebook and see if anything jumps out at you in terms of best times of day to practice, and what type of practice you really enjoy. Take a few moments to consider your experiences over the last 10 days, then begin outlining your new practice plan in your Meditation Notebook by answering these questions:

- Was there a time of day that suited your schedule best?

- What was your favorite meditation technique?

- Do you have a preferred meditation posture?

- Did any meditation stir up strong emotions?

- Was any meditation especially soothing?

Building Your Practice

Consistency is key. Missing a day or two can easily turn into missing months at a time. Keep building the habit! Even if you miss your established time in the morning (or evening or lunchtime), create some other time in the day for a quick 10-minute meditation.

Keep using your Meditation Notebook to reflect on things you notice as your practice deepens. It will also be beneficial to keep track of anything that comes up in daily living that indicates some kind of change resulting from your meditation practice. For example, did you notice that you were less reactive than usual when you received bad news? Journal about it and document some details. Were you able to experience deeper levels of appreciation for a meal you were eating? Make a note of it. Keep your Meditation Notebook around to track your progress, creative ideas, and for the occasional Writing Meditation (see Day 10: Go Deeper).

Mix it up! As I mentioned before, you could even begin this 10-day program over again. I have found that practicing different styles of meditation can keep things fresh and challenging, much like a rotating workout routine keeps the training challenging. There are numerous things to consider here, such as your meditation goals. Are you feeling stressed and looking to relax? Are you having trouble sleeping at night and hoping for deeper rest? Reflect on your journal entries and any notes from the last 10 days to help you clarify some goals.

A flexible practice is a sustainable practice. I recommend finding your unique balance between consistency and flexibility. You will want to ensure that your practice is as consistent as possible (daily, or even twice a day!), but take care not to force yourself into so rigid a schedule that if something comes up you miss it altogether. Become open to different forms of meditation. For example, if you miss a morning meditation, maybe dedicate your lunch break to mindful eating. Also, be flexible as to the duration of your sit. If you're a morning meditator and you oversleep one day, three minutes of counting your breath may be all you can manage. That's fine for that morning, and infinitely better than skipping your practice altogether. Take your three minutes, be grateful for them, and see if you can schedule another session later in the day.

Moving Forward

Committing—and recommitting—to your practice is ongoing. Like gently pulling your mind back to its focus when you meditate, you may sometimes find that you need to pull your intentions back to focus on your practice.

A **sangha**, or meditation community, can be extremely rewarding and supportive. I often recommend that students commit to a personal daily meditation practice and also find somewhere to meditate with a group once a week. Group practice keeps you accountable, consistent, and growing. If you're lucky enough to have meditation centers in your vicinity, check them out! See what resonates. Many of them are dedicated to one particular school or religion, but there are many out there definitely worth exploring.

For someone interested in something more immediate, here are some suggestions for finding or establishing a community around meditation:

10-Day Book Club Challenge Gather some friends for a book club challenge and go through this 10-Day meditation program together as a group. You can do the meditations together or separately and keep in touch online or via group text about your experiences and progress.

Standard Book Club You could also have weekly in-person book club meetings (any book you like!) at home or a local community center and include a 5- to 10-minute meditation at the beginning and the end of your meetings.

Practical Meditation Group Another option would be to have weekly or occasional meetings dedicated to discussing and practicing meditation. This could also be done for special occasions like holidays, celebrations, birthdays, the full moon, the new moon, or any periodic gathering of friends.

Meditation at Existing Groups or Meetings A few minutes of Mantra Meditation, lovingkindness, or even zazen are a great addition to community groups and team or family meetings.

For me, the only thing more powerful than implementing a daily meditation practice in my life was implementing regular group meditation practice. Group meditation has taken my understanding and my experience to a completely new level, and I've especially enjoyed the conversation and relationships that emerge from meditating with friends.

As you get more and more comfortable meditating, the practice will become a habit that's second nature to you. As you've learned during this 10-day program, meditation is a simple practice that can have powerful effects to heal and transform the body and mind. As with anything, you will get out what you put in! Congratulations on the journey you have begun to live a happier, calmer, more fulfilling life.

GLOSSARY OF KEY TERMS

affirmation: A statement of truth ("affirming that which is true") repeated either out loud or silently in the mind to support the development of a new belief or behavior

asana: A physical posture of the body when practicing meditation or yoga

beginner's mind: Zen concept of an open, curious mind, free of the limitations found in the mind of the "expert"

body scanning: An important, fundamental mindfulness meditation technique that focuses in on every area of your body, from head to toe, and explores how each part feels; also known as "sweeping the body"

breath awareness: The mental focus directed on the experience of the breath—all aspects of the inhale, exhale, the suspension between them, and all the physical sensations associated with the breath

chakra: One of seven energy centers aligned along the spinal column, each of which is related to a specific physical function of the body as well as an emotional, spiritual, or practical function in life

chakra balancing: A form of Body Scan Meditation designed to draw a connection between the functioning of different parts of the body and their associated life aspect

chanting: The audible repetition of a mantra that can be done using a speaking voice or a singing voice

cymatics: The study of sound vibration and the way different sound frequencies have a specific and controllable impact on the physical environment

direct experience: The process of taking personal action to experiment, question, or enjoy a particular practice rather than or in addition to reading about or studying it

emotional maturity: The learned ability to experience, identify, and express emotions in a way that is authentic but does not cause harm

emotional self-regulation: The ability to experience, identify, and adjust one's emotional state to avoid unhealthy emotional expression; different from emotional repression unless the emotions are never experienced or communicated in a healthy way

empath: An individual who is highly sensitive to the emotions of others

enlightenment: The complete understanding of all things beyond any doubt, illusion, confusion, or distortion of perception

field of awareness: The sphere of perception reaching in all directions around a person as far as she is able to perceive

gazing point: In an open-eye meditation, the specific point on a meditation object on which the meditator rests her eyes and continually brings her gaze back to every time the eyes wander—much like a visual mantra

heartfulness: Another word for lovingkindness or *metta*, specifically referring to mindfulness with compassion

love zone: The imaginary field of lovingkindness conjured up surrounding the meditator in a Lovingkindness Meditation

lovingkindness: The quality of unconditional love, acceptance, nonjudgment, and a hope for clarity, health, peace, and happiness for all life forms

mandala: Kaleidoscopic artwork sacred in Hinduism and other religions symbolizing the unified universe

mantra: Pali for "mind-vehicle," a word or phrase repeated silently or out loud in meditation, chanting, or in reciting prayer or affirmations

meditation object: The point of focus in a meditation that can be a physical item as in open-eye gazing meditation, or a word or phrase, as in Mantra Meditation

mental noting: The act of acknowledging thoughts, sounds, and other sensory input during a meditation; for example, "Wow, I'm really thinking a lot about work now—back to the mantra"

microchanges: Subtle, small, and various movements and adjustments happening throughout the body only perceptible through mindful awareness

mindful eating: The practice of imbuing the eating experience with mindful awareness of the appearance, texture, taste, and portion of food, as well as the physical sensations they create in the body

mindful observation: Gazing directly at an object; this can include or not include touching and examining the object

mindful walking: The practice of imbuing the act of walking with mindfulness, bringing awareness into every sensation and movement of the many moving parts of the body

mindfulness: The act of being totally aware of the present moment and all the sensory input one's body and mind are providing

mindfulness meditation: The exercise of practicing total awareness in a designated place and time

moving meditation: Bringing mindfulness into activities involving physical movement

mudra: Postures or configurations of the hands and fingers in meditation to achieve certain responses in the nervous system, such as increased concentration or relaxation; also sometimes casually called "hand yoga"

neural pathways: The system of nerves in the brain and body along which electrical impulses travel when thoughts or actions take place

no-thought: A transcendental state of awareness referred to in Zen as being the ultimate goal of meditation, where awareness is above the thinking mind, not a state in which the brain is no longer living and active

numbing agent: An unhealthy way (such as excessive eating, alcohol, drugs, and sexual behavior) to distract oneself from challenging or upsetting circumstances, thoughts, or feelings

open awareness: The practice of soft-focus meditation in expanding the field of awareness in all directions around oneself

repressed emotions: Difficult emotions that have been ignored and overlooked either by avoidance or unawareness

samadi: An enlightened state of bliss

sangha: A community of people coming together to learn about self-development, spirituality, and meditation

shavasana: The posture in which the meditator lies flat on her back with palms facing up, especially in yoga nidra or Body Scan Meditation; also known as corpse pose

soft focus: Another phrase for open awareness or open mindfulness

thoughts: The firing of electrical impulses along neural pathways in the brain as the mind automatically responds to the sensory input of the present moment as well as the processing of past experiences and imaginary or visionary ideas

transcend: Living with (but above) the circumstances of any given moment, as opposed to avoiding circumstances or repressing emotions

trataka: The traditional practice of yogic open-eye gazing meditation

true self: The essential quality of an individual free from all conditioning, judgments, and other personality qualities

yantra: Sacred mandala artwork in the Eastern traditions

yin and yang: The Eastern concept of the essential quality of duality in nature, as in spirituality and physicality, femininity and masculinity, darkness and light

yoga nidra: The body scan practice of taking the body into deep relaxation without allowing the mind to drift off to sleep

zazen: The Zen meditation practice of seated breath awareness meditation

Zen: An Eastern tradition brought to China from India 1,500 years ago by Bodhidharma; a combination of Indian Buddhism and Chinese Taoism

REFERENCES

Alexander, Ronald. *Wise Mind, Open Mind: Finding Purpose and Meaning in Times of Crisis, Loss, and Change.* Oakland, CA: New Harbinger Publications, 2009.

Decide to Drive. "Eating While Driving." Accessed November 15, 2017. https://www.decidetodrive.org/distracted-driving-dangerous/eating -driving/.

Goel, Arun. "Trataka — A Meditation Practice for Everyone." *Health and Yoga.* Accessed November 16, 2017. http://www.healthandyoga.com /html/news/meditation/trataka.aspx.

Grohol, John M. "Need to Form a New Habit? 66 Days." *World of Psychology.* Accessed November 14, 2017. https://psychcentral.com /blog/need-to-form-a-new-habit-66-days/.

Hawkins, Dr. James. "Barbara Fredrickson's Recent Research Study on Loving-Kindness Meditation (First Post)." *Good Medicine.* Last modified December 1, 2010. http://www.goodmedicine.org.uk/stressedtozest /2008/12/barbara-fredrickson%E2%80%99s-recent-research-study -loving-kindness-meditation-first-.

Hölzel, Britta K., James Carmody, Mark Vangel, Christina Congleton, Sitta M. Yerramsetti, Tim Gard, and Sara W. Lazar. "Mindfulness Practice Leads to Increases in Regional Brain Gray Matter Density." *Psychiatry Research: Neuroimaging* 191, no. 1 (January 30, 2011): Abstract. doi:10.1016/j.pscychresns.2010.08.006.

Kabat-Zinn, Jon, Ann O. Massion, Jean Kristeller, Linda G. Peterson, Kenneth E. Fletcher, Lori Pbert, William R. Lenderking, Saki F. Santorelli. "Effectiveness of a Meditation-Based Stress Reduction Program in the Treatment of Anxiety Disorders." *The American Journal of Psychiatry* 149, no. 7 (July 1992): 936–943. doi:10.1176/ajp.149.7.936.

Krishnamurti, Jiddu. *As One Is: To Free the Mind from All Conditioning.* Prescott, AZ: Hohm Press, 2007.

Kornfield, Jack. *After the Ecstasy, the Laundry: How the Heart Grows Wise on the Spiritual Path.* New York: Bantam Books, 2001.

Leuven, K. U. "Mindfulness at School Reduces (Likelihood of) Depression-Related Symptoms in Adolescents." *ScienceDaily.* March 15, 2013. www.sciencedaily.com/releases/2013/03/130315095916.htm.

Locher, Jamie, and Owen Moritz. "Eating While Driving Causes 80% of All Car Accidents, Study Shows." *NY Daily News.* July 19, 2009. Accessed November 12, 2017. http://www.nydailynews.com/new-york/eating-driving-80-car-accidents-study-shows-article-1.427796.

Luders, Eileen, Arthur W. Toga, Natasha Lepore, and Christian Gaser. "The Underlying Anatomical Correlates of Long-term Meditation: Larger Hippocampal and Frontal Volumes of Gray Matter." *NeuroImage* 45, no. 3 (April 15, 2009): 672–678. doi:10.1016/j.neuroimage.2008.12.061.

Morin, Amy. "7 Scientifically Proven Benefits of Gratitude." *Psychology Today.* April 3, 2015. https://www.psychologytoday.com/blog/what-mentally-strong-people-dont-do/201504/7-scientifically-proven-benefits-gratitude.

Moyer, Melinda Wenner. "Is Meditation Overrated?" *Scientific American.* May 1, 2014. https://www.scientificamerican.com/article/is-meditation-overrated/.

Nadrich, Ora. *Says Who?: How One Simple Question Can Change the Way You Think Forever.* New York: Morgan James Publishing, 2016.

Nhat Hanh, Thich. *Peace Is Every Step: The Path of Mindfulness in Everyday Life.* New York: Bantam Books, 2013.

Popova, Maria. "How Long It Takes to Form a New Habit." *Brain Pickings.* January 2, 2014. https://www.brainpickings.org/2014/01/02 /how-long-it-takes-to-form-a-new-habit/.

Robinson, Eric, Paul Aveyard, Amanda Daley, Kate Jolly, Amanda Lewis, Deborah Lycett, and Suzanne Higgs. "Eating Attentively: a Systematic Review and Meta-Analysis of the Effect of Food Intake Memory and Awareness on Eating." *The American Journal of Clinical Nutrition 97,* no. 4 (February 27, 2013): Abstract. doi:10.3945/ajcn.112.045245.

Schneider, Dr. Robert. "Does Meditation Have Benefits for Mind and Body?" *Medical News Today.* February 26, 2014. https:// www.medicalnewstoday.com/articles/272833.php.

Schulte, Brigid. "Harvard Neuroscientist: Meditation Not Only Reduces Stress, Here's How It Changes Your Brain." *Washington Post.* May 26, 2015. https://www.washingtonpost.com/news/inspired-life /wp/2015/05/26/harvard-neuroscientist-meditation-not-only-reduces -stress-it-literally-changes-your-brain/?utm_term=.dd361811a8e5.

Seppälä, Emma. "18 Science-Based Reasons to Try Loving-Kindness Meditation." *Mindful.* October 1, 2014. https://www.mindful.org /18-science-based-reasons-to-try-loving-kindness-meditation/.

Shapiro, Shauna L., John A. Astin, Scott R. Bishop, Matthew Cordova. "Mindfulness-Based Stress Reduction for Health Care Professionals: Results From a Randomized Trial." *International Journal of Stress Management* 12, no. 2 (May 2005): 164-176. doi:10.1037/1072-5245.12.2.164.

Suzuki, Shunryu. *Zen Mind, Beginner's Mind: Informal Talks on Zen Meditation and Practice.* Boston: Shambhala, 2011.

Watts, Alan. *The Way of Zen.* New York: Vintage Books, 1999.

Williamson, Marianne. *Tears to Triumph: The Spiritual Journey from Suffering to Enlightenment*. New York: HarperOne, 2017.

Wilson, Angela. "Loving-Kindness Meditation and Change." *HuffPost*. Last modified January 23, 2014. https://www.huffingtonpost.com /kripalu/loving-kindness-meditation_b_3961300.html.

Zeidan, Fadel, Susan K. Johnson, Bruce J. Diamond, Zhanna David, and Paula Goolkasian. "Mindfulness Meditation Improves Cognition: Evidence of Brief Mental Training." *Consciousness and Cognition* 19, no. 2 (June 2010): 597–605. doi:10.1016/j.concog.2010.03.014.

INDEX

ACKNOWLEDGMENTS

Love and honor go to my parents, Jeff and Karma Decker, my brothers, Andrew, Christopher, Chad, Scott, and Theo, my sisters-in-law, my aunts, uncles, all my wonderful cousins and grandparents, and my prodigious, miraculous, beautiful nieces and nephews for whom this book was created.

Deep respect for the mentors and teachers whom I look to every day for guidance: Ora Nadrich, Marianne Williamson, Dr. Ronald Alexander, Michael Bernard Beckwith, Lorin Roche, PhD, Tim Ryan, Nesa and Roger Weir, Trudy Goodman, HH the 14th Dalai Lama, His Holiness Pope Francis, Suze Yalof Schwartz, Daniel P. Brown, Bernie Sanders, Dr. Judith Orloff, Corey Folsom, Katherine Woodward Thomas, Chandresh Bhardwaj, Deepak Chopra, Touré Roberts, Alan Clements, and Eckhart Tolle.

Infinite gratitude for the divine support goes to Darcie Odom, Julia Nugent, Felicia Tomasko, Justin Faerman, Meghan McDonald, Jen Buonantony, Kyle Gray, Jennifer Sodini, Jeffrey Segal, Tal Rabinowitz, Megan Monahan, Colin Benward, Caitlin Crosby, Andrew Keegan, Alan Polsky, Sean Stone, Daniel Pinchbeck, Jenny Deveau, Seth Misterka, Devyn Ascher, Jillian Rose, Tom Seefried, Katlyn Skoien, Matthew Fernando, Maya Popkin, Noah Berman, Leah Santa Cruz, Wendy Zahler, Jessica Hall, Kyle Carlson, Katie Cleary, Jasmine Dustin, Katarina Van Derham, Andrew Stern, Kim Biddle, Kris Wolfe, Titus Makin Jr., Stephen Werner, AnnaLynne McCord, Linnea Miron, Katie Piel, Jeff Marinucci, Debbie Coombs, Erica Greve, Crystal Hoang, Jordan Wagner, Evan Kirkpatrick, Gerry and Brandee Powell, Deborah Brock, Christine Peake, Javier and Natalia Herrera, Chance Foreman,

Anthony Ranville, Mia Banducci, Liz Marz, Cyrus Shiahiari, Camilla Sacre-Dallerup, Cassandra Bodzak, Eben Oroz, Meredith Cohen, Racquel Tristan, Orion Solarion, Susan Stanger, Jeff and Tammy McGee, Trevor Stansbury, Paul Oakley, Kelly Corbridge, Paul Teodo, Olivia Rosewood, David Ayla, Steve Pearson, and all the many people whom I was unable to fit here.

Heartfelt thanks go to Camille Hayes, Meg Ilasco, and the whole team at Althea Press and Callisto Media.

Benjamin W. Decker is a meditation teacher and social activist in Los Angeles. He is the director of education at The Institute For Transformational Thinking and a founding teacher at Unplug Meditation, The DEN Meditation, and Wanderlust Hollywood. He is also the former director of partnerships at humanitarian aid organization Generosity.org and at anti-human trafficking organization Unlikely Heroes.

CPSIA information can be obtained
at www.ICGtesting.com
Printed in the USA
JSHW052122010222
22465JS00001B/1